Levitan, Sar A.
    Jobs for the disabled / Sar A.
Levitan and Robert Taggart. Baltimore :
Johns Hopkins University Press, c1977.
    xiii, 129 p. : ill. ; 21 cm. (Policy
studies in employment and welfare ; no.
28)

POLICY STUDIES IN EMPLOYMENT AND WELFARE NUMBER 28

General Editor: Sar A. Levitan

Jobs for the Disabled

Sar A. Levitan
and Robert Taggart

The Johns Hopkins University Press
Baltimore and London

Manufactured in the United States of America

The Johns Hopkins University Press, Baltimore, Maryland 21218
The Johns Hopkins Press Ltd., London

Library of Congress Catalog Card Number 76–49910
ISBN 0–8018–1925–3
ISBN 0–8018–1926–1 (pbk)

Library of Congress Cataloging in Publication data will be found on the last printed page of this book.

Contents

Introduction: Perspectives

Diagnosis and Prescriptions   111
   Causes and Cures   111
   Policy Considerations   117

Tables

1 Work Experience of Persons Aged 20 to 64 during 1971   4

2 Disabled as Percentage of All Persons Aged 20 to 64, by Employment Status, 1972   7

3 Incidence of Chronic Conditions and Disability, 1972   12

4 Activity Limitations among Disabled and Nondisabled, 1972   14

5 Disability Status in 1969 of Persons Disabled Less Than 10 Years in 1966   19

6 Changes in Incidence of Disability between 1966 and 1972   24

7 Employment Status of Nondisabled and of Severely and Occupationally Disabled, 1966 and 1972   25

8 Vocational Rehabilitation Activity, Fiscal 1975 and 1965   29

9 Disabled Reporting Having Received Rehabilitation Services, 1966 and 1972   30

10 Reported Sources of Rehabilitation Services Received by Disabled, 1972   31

11 Services Provided by Federal/State Vocational Rehabilitation Program, Fiscal 1975   40

12 Vocational Rehabilitation Expenditures, by Service Category, Fiscal 1975   41

13 Average Annual Earnings of 1964 Manpower Development and Training Act Enrollees and Controls, 1962 to 1969   80

Figures

Introduction

One in seven noninstitutionalized adult Americans aged 20 through 64 years is afflicted with chronic conditions lasting six or more months that limit the kind or amount of work he or she can perform. The consequences of these work disabilities are serious for individuals and for society: earnings are curtailed or eliminated, and income is lowered. Only two-fifths of the disabled are employed during a typical year, compared with three-fourths of the nondisabled. The mean annual earnings of disabled workers are roughly seven-tenths those of the non-disabled, and a household with a disabled adult must make do with a third less income than other households. Behind these numbers lie untold personal tribulations resulting from the loss of work status and independence.

The costs to society also are considerable. The economy suffers to the extent that useful skills go unutilized. Relatives must supplement the reduced earnings of disabled persons while bearing extra medical and personal-care expenses. Tax-payers support extensive income transfers.

Vocational rehabilitation seeks to restore lost or stunted productivity, thereby increasing the earnings, the indepen-dence, and the well-being of the disabled and reducing the need for public income transfers. To achieve these goals medical, prosthetic, psychological, and other services that treat the mental and physical handicaps are combined with counseling, vocational training, work experience, placement, and other services that address the temporary or long-term employment problems related to these handicaps. In 1975 an estimated $1.7 billion was spent on such services under the major public programs.

Work disability and vocational rehabilitation services cannot be considered in a vacuum. Many of the socioeconomically handicapped have complicating mental or physical problems, and a large proportion of those with mental or physical handicaps have limited education, little work experience, or other impediments to employment.

There is also an overlap between vocational rehabilitation and the other employment and training efforts for the disadvantaged. Although the rehabilitation and manpower camps have maintained their distance, vocational rehabilitation programs serve some whose difficulties are more socioeconomic than physical, and general manpower programs sometimes provide medical services and help to the handicapped. Manpower and vocational rehabilitation programs face the same sets of problems and must resolve the same issues in serving their clients: the fundamental constraints, at least in the short run, are the lack of jobs for those at the end of the pecking order, the multiple handicaps of those in need, and the overlap with the income transfer system, which may make employment unprofitable.

Both manpower and vocational rehabilitation policymakers must decide whether to concentrate on developing human resources or on trying to change labor markets. A choice must be made between serving the most handicapped in any client group—thus risking a lower success rate—and selecting the less disabled, who do not need help as much. A balance must be reached between securing "good" jobs, which are limited in number but offer major economic improvements, and settling for "bad" jobs, which are more readily available but result in lesser benefits. There is a related question of whether scarce resources should be spread thinly to try to do something for everyone or concentrated to achieve significant gains for a smaller number. Should jobs be created, or are jobs available once the disadvantaged or disabled are made more employable?

Since they have similar aims and operate within similar constraints, vocational rehabilitation and manpower programs can be judged in part by many of the same standards. Do services improve the employment and earnings of participants? Do services change the behavior of clients, favorably affecting their attitudes and increasing constructive activities? Will increased self-support reduce the demand for income maintenance? Do the program benefits outweigh the costs?

Despite these obvious parallels, vocational rehabilitation programs for the disabled and employment and training efforts for the socioeconomically handicapped have, for the most part, run on separate tracks. The problems of the disabled have been conceptualized and measured from a medical perspective. Vocational rehabilitation programs have paid little attention to labor markets, on the assumption that jobs would be available once lost functions were restored. Moreover, the performance of vocational rehabilitation programs has never been given the same close scrutiny as that of manpower efforts. The latter have been condemned because, in the numerous studies of their effectiveness, inadequacies in selection of control groups and other problems have raised doubts about the generally favorable findings. Yet in the far fewer evaluations of vocational rehabilitation, control groups have rarely been used. Although it has long been suspected that the most employable disabled are selected for rehabilitation (a process known as "creaming"), there has been little progress in determining how much it influences the positive outcomes.

The less demanding standards applied to vocational rehabilitation reflect a pervasive notion that the disabled are somehow more "deserving" than the socioeconomically disadvantaged, and this is manifested elsewhere. For instance, the explosive growth of Aid to Families with Dependent Children (AFDC) in the 1960s generated a great deal of concern and debate about workfare versus welfare; rapid growth of disability programs generated far less rancor and much less concern with the question of employability. In the early 1970s doubts about human resource development efforts resulted in budget cuts for manpower programs and overhaul of the delivery systems. Meanwhile, vocational rehabilitation activities continued to grow and prosper undisturbed.

The vocational rehabilitation and manpower establishments have kept at arm's length and have resolved issues in very different ways. In response to the severe recession of the 1970s, manpower policy shifted dramatically away from training to job creation; the clientele of manpower programs also changed noticeably, with increased emphasis on the less disadvantaged who were out of work because of the recession. Meanwhile, there was little change in vocational rehabilitation approaches. Priorities were shifted to serving the more, rather than the less, severely handicapped.

Vocational rehabilitation efforts have been immune from the critical scrutiny leveled at other human resource investments, but a day of reckoning may be at hand. The burden of proof for social welfare spending has increased. Income transfers to the disabled have been growing rapidly, and workfare versus welfare issues are bound to surface as costs mount. A rapid rise in the number of persons unable to work regularly or at all, despite improved care and services, will inevitably attract attention. The performance of vocational rehabilitation programs has deteriorated in the slack labor markets of the 1970s.

To avoid excessive criticism, to adjust to changing conditions, and to move toward greater consistency or at least toward mutual understanding between manpower and rehabilitation efforts, it would be useful to apply manpower perspectives and performance standards to vocational rehabilitation efforts. This application would have to begin with an emphasis on the realities of the labor market and on the strategies directly related to improving employability and job openings. Performance would be judged primarily in terms of employment and earnings gains, with the issues of creaming and control-group inadequacy faced head on. The differences between manpower policies and vocational rehabilitation policies would have to be justified.

Such an emphasis on employment and training does not mean that medical and related treatments are unimportant or that there are no major benefits besides increased earnings. Consideration of vocational rehabilitation from the manpower perspective does not imply that this viewpoint is "correct" or all-encompassing; it does not mean that homogeneous policies and delivery institutions are necessary or desirable. There is much, in fact, that the manpower establishment and policy-makers could learn from vocational rehabilitation, beginning with the individualized, carte blanche treatment approach, the recognition of noneconomic benefits, and the fundamental belief that those with problems deserve help. Yet vocational rehabilitators and policymakers might also benefit from stepping back and looking at their efforts as part of a larger problem and a broader commitment.

This study is part of a wide-ranging review of vocational rehabilitation undertaken by the Mershon Center of the Ohio State University and funded by the U.S. Department of Health, Education and Welfare. Responsibility for the preparation and publication of this volume was left completely to the authors.

1
Disability and Employability

Employment Problems of the Disabled

There are essentially two interrelated dimensions of work disability: the presence or perception of physical or mental handicaps and a reduced work capacity. The Social Security Act defines disability narrowly, limiting benefits to the most severe cases. A disability is the "inability to engage in any substantial gainful activity by reason of any medically determinable physical or mental impairment which can be expected to result in death or has lasted or can be expected to last for a continuous period of not less than 12 months." The Social Security Administration in its surveys of the disabled in 1966 and 1972 has defined disability much less restrictively as a limitation in the kind or amount of work (including housework) that a person can perform, resulting from a chronic condition lasting six months or longer. Under this definition the physical or mental conditions are self-assessed rather than medically determined, and they may be of shorter duration. Most important, this definition includes not only those unable to work regularly or at all, who are classified as "severely disabled," but also those who must change their line of work, that is, the "occupationally disabled," as well as those who can continue in the same job but are limited in the amount of work (including housework) they can perform—persons considered to have "secondary work limitations." The Social Security Act's definition encompasses about 3 million adults under the age of 65 years. (About 2.5 million disabled workers were receiving disability benefits at the end of 1975.) In contrast, the 1972 survey of the disabled counted 7.7 million severely disabled persons aged 20 to 64 years, 3.5 million occupationally disabled, and 4.4 million with secondary work limitations.

Employment Problems

The extent of work limitation ranges from complete to very marginal. Only a seventh of the severely disabled were employed at the time of the 1972 survey, and only 6 percent held full-time jobs (figure 1). The occupationally disabled were substantially better off, with 71 percent employed and 45 percent in full-time jobs; however, they were still worse off than the nondisabled population, among whom 74 percent were employed, 61 percent in full-time jobs. Severely disabled males had one-fifth the chance of being employed as the nondisabled, and less than one-seventh the probability of being employed full-time. Occupationally disabled males were employed somewhat less than the nondisabled but had twice the frequency of part-time work. Only one in ten severely disabled females engaged in gainful employment. Occupationally disabled women were usually forced into part-time work. The category of secondary work limitation is difficult to interpret for females because it includes women who cannot perform housework as well as those who are or would be in the labor force.

The disabled are subject to frequent work interruptions. In 1971, 72 percent of disabled males aged 20 to 64 held jobs, compared with 98 percent of the nondisabled. But 73 percent of the nondisabled, compared with only 36 percent of the disabled, had full-time, full-year jobs (table 1).

The employment problems of the disabled have other dimensions. At the time of the 1972 interview 37 percent of the severely disabled who claimed to be employed were not currently on the job, compared with just one in eight of the nondisabled

Figure 1. Employment Status of Persons Aged 20 to 64, 1972

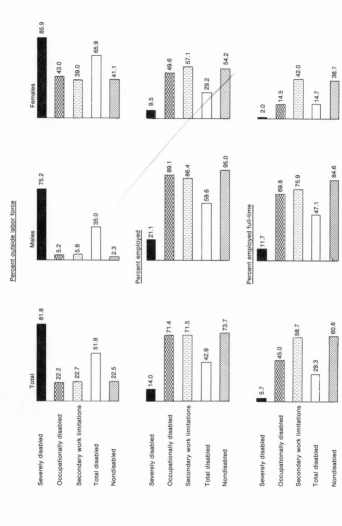

Percent outside labor force

	Total	Males	Females
Severely disabled	81.8	75.2	85.9
Occupationally disabled	22.2	5.2	43.0
Secondary work limitations	22.7	5.8	39.0
Total disabled	51.9	35.0	65.9
Nondisabled	22.5	2.3	41.1

Percent employed

	Total	Males	Females
Severely disabled	14.0	21.1	9.5
Occupationally disabled	71.4	89.1	49.6
Secondary work limitations	71.5	86.4	57.1
Total disabled	42.9	59.6	29.2
Nondisabled	73.7	95.0	54.2

Percent employed full-time

	Total	Males	Females
Severely disabled	5.7	11.7	2.0
Occupationally disabled	45.0	69.8	14.5
Secondary work limitations	58.7	75.9	42.0
Total disabled	29.3	47.1	14.7
Nondisabled	60.6	84.6	38.7

SOURCE: Social Security Administration, U.S. Department of Health, Education and Welfare, 1972 survey of the disabled, unpublished tabulations.

Table 1. Work Experience of Persons Aged 20 to 64 during 1971 (percent)

Work experience	Nondisabled	Disabled Total	Severely disabled	Occupationally disabled	Secondary work limitations
Total					
Did not work	20.7	45.8	69.5	21.1	23.5
Worked	79.1	54.1	30.3	78.9	76.5
Full time, 50–52 weeks	50.4	22.7	5.4	37.7	41.5
Full time, 26–49 weeks	12.1	11.9	6.8	14.7	18.8
Part time, 26 or more weeks	8.1	8.1	6.6	14.2	5.9
Less than 26 weeks	6.3	9.4	10.0	9.3	8.1
Not available	2.2	2.0	1.5	3.0	2.2
Not available	0.2	0.1	0.2	—	—
Male					
Did not work	2.3	27.7	56.1	7.2	6.5
Worked	97.5	72.2	43.7	92.8	93.5
Full time, 50–52 weeks	72.9	35.6	10.0	54.0	54.6
Full time, 26–49 weeks	13.7	19.2	13.8	22.0	24.3
Part time, 26 or more weeks	4.0	5.7	5.5	8.0	3.7
Less than 26 weeks	4.1	9.1	12.0	5.4	8.4
Not available	2.8	2.6	2.3	3.4	2.4
Not available	0.2	0.2	0.2	—	0.1
Female					
Did not work	37.5	60.8	77.9	38.1	39.9
Worked	62.3	39.2	22.0	61.9	60.0
Full time, 50–52 weeks	29.9	12.1	2.5	17.6	28.9
Full time, 26–49 weeks	10.6	5.9	2.4	5.8	13.5
Part time, 26 or more weeks	11.9	10.1	7.2	21.8	8.0
Less than 26 weeks	8.3	9.5	8.8	14.2	7.9
Not available	1.7	1.6	1.2	2.5	1.7
Not available	0.1	0.1	0.1	—	—

SOURCE: Social Security Administration, U.S. Department of Health, Education and Welfare, 1972 survey of the disabled, unpublished tabulations.

with a job. The employed nondisabled averaged forty-one hours of work weekly; the severely disabled averaged twenty-six and the occupationally disabled thirty-six hours. The disabled who found employment were concentrated in the worst jobs (figure 2). Accounting for a tenth of the work force, the disabled were a sixth of all service workers, laborers, and farmers and more than a third of all private household workers. The weekly wage of employed disabled males averaged 79 percent that of the nondisabled; for the severely disabled it was only 67 percent. The ratios for females were even lower, 74 and 46 percent respectively. Because of more frequently interrupted work, the annual earnings of disabled males with work experience were 69 percent those of the nondisabled; the severely disabled earned less than half as much, the occupationally disabled, 70 percent, and persons with secondary work limitations, 79 percent as much as the nondisabled.

Nearly three in every ten persons aged 20 to 64 not in the labor force—without jobs and not looking for work—at the time of the 1972 survey were disabled, including seven in ten working-age males (table 2). Conversely, less than 8 percent of all full-time workers were limited in the kind or amount of work they could perform. With unemployment rates twice those of the nondisabled, disabled men accounted for a fourth of jobless men. Disabled women, on the other hand, apparently dropped out of or did not enter the labor market rather than pursue a futile search for work, so their unemployment rates differed little from those of nondisabled women. Whereas the disabled represented 28 percent of all persons who did not work during 1971 and a fifth of those who worked less than twenty-six weeks, they accounted for 8 percent of full-time, full-year workers. Two-thirds of males who did not work and more than a fourth of those with less than twenty-six weeks of employment were disabled.

Characteristics

The young and the old, nonwhites, women, the unmarried, and persons with less education are overrepresented among

5

Figure 2. Occupational Distribution of Employed Disabled and Nondisabled
Workers, 1972

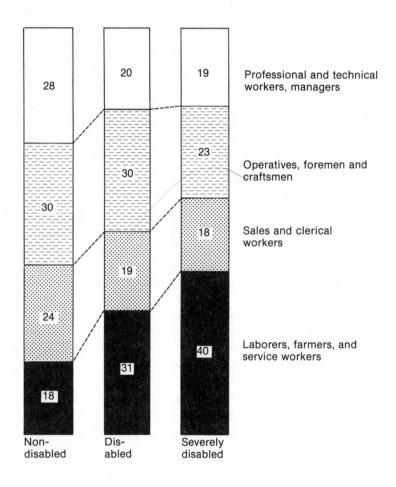

SOURCE: Social Security Administration, U.S. Department of Health, Education and Welfare, 1972 survey of the disabled, unpublished tabulations.

Table 2. Disabled as Percentage of All Persons Aged 20 to 64,
by Employment Status, 1972

	Percentage disabled	Percentage severely disabled
All persons aged 20 to 64	*14.6*	*7.3*
Not in labor force	28.3	22.2
In labor force	9.5	1.7
Employed	9.1	1.5
Full time	7.7	0.7
Part time	15.7	4.8
Unemployed	18.2	6.7
Male	*14.0*	*5.9*
Not in labor force	71.2	64.7
In labor force	9.7	1.5
Employed	9.2	1.4
Full time	8.3	0.9
Part time	17.6	5.8
Unemployed	24.5	5.7
Female	*15.2*	*8.5*
Not in labor force	22.4	16.3
In labor force	9.3	2.1
Employed	8.8	1.6
Full time	6.4	0.5
Part time	14.6	4.2
Unemployed	14.5	7.3

SOURCE: Social Security Administration, U.S. Department of Health, Education and Welfare, 1972 survey of the disabled, unpublished tabulations.

persons without jobs or without stable employment as well as among the disabled. The mentally and physically handicapped with such characteristics are more frequently unable to work regularly or at all than the less disadvantaged disabled. By the same token, the employment problems of the aged, of non-whites, and of the poorly educated are very often related to mental or physical problems, as shown in the following 1972 figures:

1. *Age*—A third of all persons aged 60 to 64 and a fourth of those aged 55 to 59 were disabled, compared with one in ten among 35- to 44-year-olds. Persons aged 55 to 64 represented only a sixth of nondisabled adults, but they accounted for 36 percent of the disabled. Finally, two-thirds of disabled persons aged 55 and over were unable to work regularly or at all, compared with only two-fifths of younger persons with disabilities.

2. *Race*—Blacks, who represented 9 percent of nondisabled adults in 1972, accounted for 14 percent of the disabled and 16 percent of the severely disabled. Among blacks with a disability 58 percent could not work regularly or at all, compared with 48 percent among whites with a disability.

3. *Sex and marital status*—The incidence of disability was only slightly higher among women than among men, but 56 percent of disabled females, compared with only 42 percent of disabled males, were unable to work regularly or at all. Marital status was also a factor. Among the nondisabled only 9 percent of adults were widowed, divorced, or separated; the proportion among the disabled was twice as high.

4. *Education*—Whereas seven of ten nondisabled adults had at least a high school diploma in 1972, only 44 percent of the disabled and less than a third of the severely disabled were high school graduates or better. A third of all persons with eight grades or less of education and nearly a fifth of high school dropouts were disabled, compared with only 8 percent of those with some college education. Nearly two-thirds of the disabled with eight grades or less of education could not work regularly or at all, compared with two-fifths of disabled high school graduates and three-tenths of those with some college training.

The compounding of mental or physical and socioeconomic handicaps reduces the chances of labor market success. Those who are both disadvantaged and disabled are more likely to have severe employment problems than any other group. The earnings of disabled white males aged 45 to 54 were two-fifths those of the nondisabled. Disabled black males in the same age bracket earned only one-fourth as much; disabled black females, 8 percent (figure 3).

Employer surveys evidence a general reluctance to hire the disabled when nondisabled workers are available. Many employers believe that there are higher costs, such as increased workers' compensation expenses or inflated medical and life insurance premiums. Although most believe that the disabled will be more reliable, they fear involuntary absenteeism and turnover. Another consideration is the lack of flexibility in job assignments and the difficulty of promoting.[1] One recent study

8

Figure 3. Average Earnings of Disabled and Nondisabled Persons, 1969

Earnings as percent of disabled white males aged 45 to 54

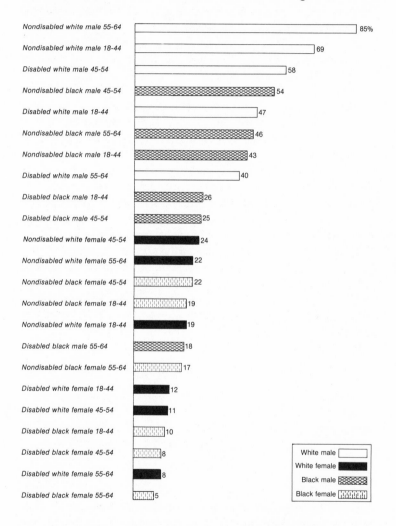

SOURCE: U.S. Bureau of the Census, *Persons With Work Disability,* PC(2)-6C (Washington: U.S. Government Printing Office, 1973), table 9.

asked Los Angeles employers to rank various groups in the order in which they believed most other firms would be likely to hire them. The mentally ill and the retarded, followed by alcoholics and drug addicts, were found to be the least attractive workers. The physically disabled were next in line, ranked below minority groups, older workers, and ex-offenders.[2]

A number of studies of the job performance of the disabled have sought to prove that these views are irrational and discriminatory. Yet the performance of the carefully screened disabled persons who find work is not necessarily indicative of the potential of others. Moreover, the existence of a few productive employment opportunities for disabled workers does not prove that there is a large number of additional jobs they could fill. Whether based on reasonable best guesses by employers or on an unreasoned bias against the mentally and physically handicapped, the attitudes are facts of life that will be difficult to change. Publicity campaigns to encourage the hiring of the disabled have not met with much success.[3]

Thus, both supply and demand factors are involved in the employment problems of the disabled. Those with disabilities very frequently have other work impediments, such as old age or limited education, and the presence of a physical or mental condition is itself a handicap both to working and to finding or holding a job.

The Interaction of Socioeconomic and Physical Handicaps

By definition, the disabled are those who have chronic conditions lasting six months or more. The incidence and severity of disability are affected by the kind and number of afflictions and by the functional limitations that result.

Incidence of Interactions

In 1972 almost half of all noninstitutionalized adults aged 20 to 64 reported suffering from one or more chronic conditions. However, only 30 percent of these were limited in the kind or amount of work they could perform, and just 15 percent were unable to work regularly or at all. What made a chronic condition a disabling one? The incidence of disability and severe disability varied by condition. Only three in ten persons with varicose veins, a third of those with deafness and, perhaps surprisingly, a fourth of those missing arms or hands, were limited in the kind or amount of work they could perform (table 3). Even smaller proportions of persons with these conditions could not work regularly or at all. In contrast, 96 percent of mentally retarded adults had work limitations, as did 89 percent of those with multiple sclerosis, 84 percent of stroke victims, 80 percent of the mentally ill, and 73 percent of those with epilepsy; more than six in ten with such conditions could not work regularly or at all.

The disabled, especially the severely disabled, were more likely than the nondisabled with chronic conditions to suffer from these more serious problems. Nevertheless, the most prevalent causes of disability were arthritis and rheumatism, trouble with the back or spine, high blood pressure, heart trouble, and chronic nerves, inflictions that are suffered by many without resulting in work limitations. Of the broader categories, musculo-skeletal problems were present among three-fifths of the disabled and cardiovascular difficulties among half.

The compounding of unfavorable conditions frequently results in disability. Whereas only 6 percent of the nondisabled reported three or more chronic conditions, over half of the disabled were plagued by multiple maladies. Arthritis or a nervous disorder alone might not greatly limit work, but combined with high blood pressure or thyroid problems it might create severe impediments. The incidence of multiple conditions increases with age, and this is one of the reasons for the correlation between age and disability.

Severe and multiple conditions reduce the capacity to function physically and emotionally, while the discomforting symptoms may lessen work motivation. About four-fifths of the disabled in 1972 suffered from some physical limitation: two-fifths had trouble walking, three-fifths in lifting more than ten pounds; half could not stand for long periods or had difficulty

11

Table 3. Incidence of Chronic Conditions and Disability, 1972*

Kind of condition	Percentage with condition who are disabled	Percentage with condition who are severely disabled	Percentage of nondisabled with condition	Percentage of disabled with condition	Percentage of severely disabled with condition
Musculo-skeletal	*45*	*23*	*13*	*61*	*61*
Arthritis/rheumatism	44	25	7	33	37
Back or spine trouble	50	22	6	33	29
Missing legs or feet	79	41	–	1	1
Missing arms or hands	25	6	–	–	–
Chronic stiffness	61	34	2	12	14
Cardiovascular	*37*	*21*	*15*	*50*	*59*
Rheumatic fever	46	26	–	2	2
Heart attacks	73	50	–	6	9
Heart trouble	68	45	1	14	20
Stroke	84	74	–	3	4
Hardening of arteries	62	45	–	4	6
High blood pressure	42	26	5	22	27
Varicose veins	30	15	4	9	9
Hemorrhoids	24	12	6	10	11
Respiratory	*38*	*20*	*8*	*27*	*29*
Tuberculosis	63	41	1	1	2
Bronchitis	53	36	–	7	9
Emphysema	62	38	1	5	6
Asthma	38	17	2	8	8
Allergies	29	12	4	10	9
Digestive	*39*	*22*	*6*	*22*	*25*
Gall bladder	50	32	1	4	6
Stomach ulcer	34	20	3	8	10
Hernia	38	16	1	5	4

Table 3 (continued)

Kind of condition	Percentage with condition who are disabled	Percentage with condition who are severely disabled	Percentage of nondisabled with condition	Percentage of disabled with condition	Percentage of severely disabled with condition
Mental	64	46	2	20	29
Mental illness	80	72	—	3	6
Mental retardation	96	77	—	2	3
Alcohol/drugs	47	20	—	1	1
Chronic nerves	62	43	2	15	22
Nervous system	81	62	—	4	6
Epilepsy	73	60	—	2	4
Multiple sclerosis	89	79	—	1	1
Urogenital	46	26	2	7	8
Kidney	43	27	2	6	8
Neoplasm	42	26	2	7	9
Tumor or cyst	35	21	1	4	5
Cancer	64	43	—	3	4
Endocrine	33	20	4	10	13
Diabetes	47	29	1	7	8
Thyroid	22	13	2	4	4
Auditory	36	18	2	5	5
Visual	66	40	1	6	7

SOURCE: Social Security Administration, U.S. Department of Health, Education and Welfare, 1972 survey of the disabled, unpublished tabulations.

* Incidences of less than 0.5 percent are not included.

stooping and kneeling (table 4). The majority of persons with such physical impairments were disabled, especially those who had trouble walking or reaching. The disabled also were more frequently the victims of multiple limitations. A third had five or more, compared with less than 2 percent of the nondisabled population. Eight in ten persons reporting five or more physical limitations were limited in the kind or amount of work they could perform.

Table 4. Activity Limitations among Disabled and Nondisabled,
1972 (percent)

Limitation	Nondisabled	Total disabled	Severely disabled
None	86	21	11
Some	14	79	89
Walking	3	41	58
Using stairs	3	42	60
Standing long periods	6	50	66
Sitting long periods	3	30	43
Stooping or kneeling	5	49	63
Lifting less than 10 pounds	2	33	50
Lifting more than 10 pounds	6	59	75
Reaching	2	29	43
Handling or fingering	2	21	32

SOURCE: Social Security Administration, U.S. Department of Health, Education and Welfare, 1972 survey of the disabled, unpublished tabulations.

These limitations are self-assessed but apparently realistic. A study comparing physicians' and patients' assessments of physical capacity found agreement on the presence or absence of a limitation in between two-thirds and three-fourths of the cases. The employed tended to overestimate and the unemployed to understate their capacities; transfer recipients were likely to consider themselves more limited than their doctors' diagnoses would indicate.[4] Quite clearly, then, the chronic conditions and their effects are real and serious in most cases. The disabled cannot function as well as the nondisabled, and the severely disabled, who are unable to work regularly or at all, tend to have the most frequent and severe problems. Yet the fact remains that many with serious conditions or multiple functional handicaps are able to work, while large numbers of persons with less severe problems claim to be disabled.

Overlapping Difficulties

The extent to which a condition or limitation is disabling depends on the work experience, demographic characteristics, and personal attributes of the individual. For instance, the white-collar worker with lower back pains or high blood pressure might be able to continue employment, whereas a laborer could not. A person whose employment options were limited to low-wage menial jobs would be more likely to give up, claim disability, and live on transfers. The man who has worked on construction jobs for thirty years is much more likely to have physical problems than the man who has worked at a desk.

Determining the relative importance of physical or mental and socioeconomic factors is basic to successfully prescribing services for an individual. In the aggregate, scarce resources must be allocated between medical treatments, employment and training services, and direct transfers depending on their relative effectiveness in overcoming impediments among members of the target groups.

Work disability results from the interaction of a number of factors, and there is no doubt that functional limitations are crucial. In 1966, 81 percent of disabled males with no functional limitations were employed, compared with 71 percent of those with minor or moderate limitations and 45 percent of the severely limited and dependent.[5] Yet the chances of being unable to work regularly or at all were also affected by age, sex, education, and previous employment. Among the disabled with only minor restrictions, 11 percent of males aged 18 to 44 were unable to work regularly or at all, compared with 34 percent of males aged 55 to 64. Two-fifths of the disabled having minor or moderate limitations and less than nine years of education were severely disabled, compared with 22 percent of high school graduates.

Regression analysis does not help much to sort out these factors. According to a study using 1966 data, functional limitations alone explained only 13 percent of the variance in severe disability among disabled males and 8 percent among females. Age alone explained 4 and 2 percent respectively for the two sexes, and education explained 6 and 3 percent respectively.[6]

15

More complex regression equations including different health and limitation variables, marital status, area unemployment, and the presence of income support were able to explain roughly half of the variance in labor force participation for white and black males.[7] But this greater explanatory power was in part the result of running separate regressions for different age, race, and sex cohorts. Another study used data from a 1972 survey of 6,493 households. Its regressions, including scaled assessments of physical, emotional, and health conditions plus age, sex, race, and education, explained only 38 percent of the variance in work disability.[8]

Better specification of socioeconomic variables, of disabling conditions, and of functional limitations might improve the understanding of these complex relationships. At present there is no way to untangle the Gordion knot of interacting factors to explain why 15.6 million American adults are (or perceive themselves to be) limited in the type or amount of work they can perform. Some general observations seem warranted, however.

First, some of the common stereotypes of the disabled are inappropriate. Disability is often associated with visible physical or mental impairments and complete dependency; on this basis, elimination of the disabling conditions is the obvious way to improve employability. These notions are contradicted by the evidence that many of the disabled have only minor or moderate limitations and that many persons afflicted with similar conditions are not limited in the kind or amount of work they can perform. Mental or physical conditions are only one factor in determining the incidence and severity of work disability, and medical treatment alone is not always a necessary—and in a majority of cases is not a sufficient—condition for restoring employability.

Second, physical or mental and socioeconomic handicaps overlap. Chronic conditions frequently affect the disadvantaged, and when they do, the result usually is more severe employment problems.

Third, although neither chronic conditions nor socioeconomic handicaps alone explain much of the variance in the incidence or severity of disability, there still is justification for either medical or manpower services. A substantial minority of the disabled can get work if they can merely overcome their physical or mental problems, and a substantial number can work despite these problems if their employability can be upgraded.

Fourth, labor market factors clearly influence the extent and severity of disability. The number of persons with chronic conditions remains roughly constant, but the proportion of those with employment problems changes with labor market developments. Income support programs also have an independent effect. Public policy can alter economic conditions and income support programs, but it can do little about the incidence of disability. Focus on labor market developments and on the impact of income maintenance programs is, therefore, crucial in understanding and dealing with disability.

The Longitudinal Perspective

Certainly the statistical interrelationships between chronic conditions, functional limitations, socioeconomic handicaps and employment problems at a given time are important; yet it is vital also to recognize the dynamic aspects of disability. Many of the disabled have been out of the labor force for years, and for them work is not a realistic option. Others are only transitionally disabled; either their physical or employment problems can be expected to be overcome with time. The remainder may benefit from assistance to accomplish gains that would otherwise not be realized. The disabled population is constantly changing, with an inflow of newly disabled, an outflow of recoverees, and gains and setbacks for those who remain handicapped.

Stocks and Flows

Whereas the overall incidence of disability increases with age, the chances of *becoming* disabled are much more evenly distributed among age cohorts.[9] The chronic conditions eventually resulting in disability have different incidence patterns. Musculo-skeletal disorders, which tend to occur in the prime working years, accounted for 37 percent of the disabling

17

conditions beginning between the ages of 18 and 34 and for 32 percent of those occurring between 35 and 54, compared with only 22 percent beginning earlier and 26 percent later. Cardiovascular disorders become more frequent with age; these accounted for 30 percent of disabilities beginning between the ages of 35 and 54 and 40 percent of those between 55 and 64. Respiratory, mental, and nervous system disorders tend to have an early incidence; they represented 43 percent of disabilities beginning before the age of 18 but only 13 percent of those beginning at 55 or older.[10]

Age is a major factor in the chances of complete or partial recovery. Those who are impaired earlier in life are more likely to improve their status or to recover completely. A 1969 follow-up of persons disabled less than ten years in 1966 found that 12 percent of males aged 18 to 44 reported recovery, compared with only 5 percent among 55- to 64-year-olds (table 5).

The chances of improvement in disability status or of complete recovery are also related to the severity of the physical and socioeconomic handicaps. For instance, among those disabled less than ten years in 1966, who had no functional limitations, 59 percent had improved, recovered, or probably recovered by 1969. The improvement rate among those with three or more limitations was 33 percent, and less than one in ten of the functionally dependent improved. A third of the disabled with less than an eighth-grade education were severely disabled in 1966; the incidence had risen to three-fifths for this cohort three years later. Among high school graduates the proportion rose only from a fifth to two-fifths. Because the less seriously handicapped are more likely to recover, data for a particular time tend to understate the number of less severely handicapped who experience disability only temporarily.

Work Adjustments

The impact of chronic conditions on employment varies over time for persons with different characteristics. The onset of disability is usually, but not always, reflected in declining employment. Among persons who became disabled between

Table 5. Disability Status in 1969 of Persons Disabled Less Than 10 Years in 1966 (percent)

	Stayed severely disabled	Became severely disabled	Stayed partially disabled	Became partially disabled	Reported recovery	Presumed recovered*
Men						
18–44	10	6	37	2	12	33
45–54	16	14	30	2	8	29
55–64	27	29	13	4	5	23
Women						
18–44	20	15	12	5	11	37
45–54	22	26	12	4	9	28
55–64	35	31	8	4	2	20
Educational attainment						
Less than 8 years	32	29	12	3	4	21
Eight years	26	27	18	2	5	23
High school dropout	23	14	19	3	7	34
Completed high school	15	23	15	5	9	33
Some college	11	8	27	2	16	36

SOURCE: Social Security Administration, U.S. Department of Health Education and Welfare, "Disability Survey, 1969, Follow-up of Disabled Adults," unpublished tabulations.

* Many of those who were reported as disabled in 1966 were reported in 1969 as not having been disabled earlier. These persons had attributes very close to those of others who recovered, so most of them can be assumed to be persons with partial disabilities in 1966 who recovered by 1969.

October 1969 and March 1971, 85 percent of the males and 60 percent of the females had been employed at onset, but a third of these had not returned to work by the survey date in the summer of 1971. A fourth of previously employed men continued working for the same employer despite the disability, and 37 percent returned after a temporary absence; only 7 percent changed employers. Even more dramatic was the finding that 95 percent of the women who continued working or returned to work stayed with the same employer. [11]

The disabled continuing or returning to work had to make adjustments, however. Two-thirds reported some change, such as doing less heavy work, resting more often, taking it easier on the job, or working fewer hours. Yet only 7 percent were given special equipment, and only 4 percent learned a new skill or trade. [12]

Employment immediately before and soon after disability is, of course, indicative of longer term work status. For the disabled population counted in the 1966 survey, the mean duration since onset was eight years. Seven of ten disabled males who had been employed in the year before the onset of their condition were working in 1966, compared with six in ten of those who had not been employed. Among women 44 percent of those working before onset were employed in 1966, compared with 19 percent of those not previously working. Again, a key factor was the ability to return to the same job. Two-thirds of the men who had been employed at onset of disability stayed with or returned to the same job; 16 percent found another one, and 18 percent did not look or did not find a job. Among women 56 percent stayed or returned, 34 percent quit looking, and only 10 percent found another job. Occupation at onset influenced the rates of continuing or returning. For males, 87 percent of farmers and farm managers, 84 percent of sales workers, and 80 percent of clerical workers continued with or returned to the same job, compared with 67 percent of all males employed at onset. Women who were farmers or farm laborers also were more likely than other women to return to the same job. [13]

Over time the chances of employment decline. Among persons disabled less than ten years who were employed in

1966, only 78 percent of males and 71 percent of females were still working in 1969. The decline in employment among the disabled under the age of 45 was 15 percent, compared with 43 percent among 55- to 64-year-old workers. Among the severely disabled holding jobs in 1966, half of the men and a third of the women remained employed in 1969. Meanwhile, less than one in eight of the disabled not in the labor force in 1966 had found employment three years later. Since recovery rates were highest for those employed in 1966, employment dropped from 47 percent among the disabled in 1966 to 28 percent among members of the cohort remaining disabled in 1969.[14]

The longer run patterns can only be surmised based on cross-sectional data, and any conclusions are therefore extremely tentative. One would expect that, after the initial disruptive impact of the disabling condition, adjustments could be made and employment increased. But as time passes, the underlying chronic conditions more frequently deteriorate than improve, and work becomes more burdensome. Apparently the balance of these forces is different for males than for females. Within each age cohort, males disabled for a year have a lower rate of employment than those with longer term disabilities. Among females the employment rate continues downward as the duration of disability lengthens (figure 4). These data, of course, understate the extent of adjustment for both sexes, since the recovered, who are more likely to be employed, leave the disabled category. It is also important to note the independent effects of age. Where as two-thirds of males aged 45 to 54 with a disability of 5 to 9 years' duration are employed, the proportion among those aged 55 to 64 is 42 percent. In other words, the increasing physical impairments or job-finding problems that are associated with greater age might offset successful adjustments.

While longer run patterns remain a matter of conjecture, it is clear that the disabled are not a static population group but rather one in constant flux, with inflows of newly disabled, outflows resulting from recovery, death, or retirement, and a good deal of fluctuation in the severity of physical and employment problems. In deciding who can and should be

Figure 4. Employment Rates, by Duration of Disability, 1970

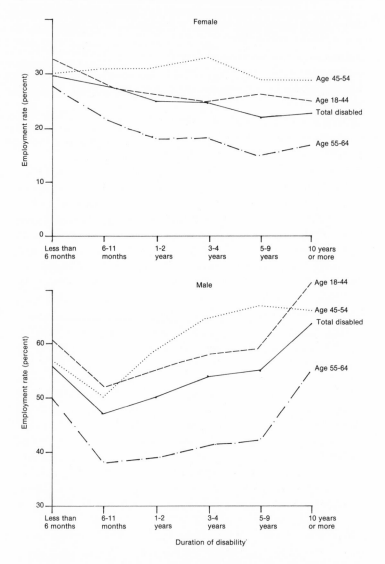

SOURCE: U.S. Bureau of the Census, *Persons with Work Disability,* PC(2)-6C (Washington: U.S. Government Printing Office, 1973), pp. 47–53.

helped, the chances of improvement or recovery with and without aid are critical issues. Lower age, better education, and male sex all are strongly related to higher rates of improvement and recovery. Work before onset is a major determinant of work afterward. A majority of those who eventually become employed after being disabled return to the same jobs, and those who do not more often remain outside the labor force than find other employment.

The Disabled in a Changing Labor Market

The disabled are disproportionately affected by labor market changes. In good times, employers are more willing to retain workers who have suffered some loss in productivity and to hire those for whom some adjustments may be necessary. In bad times, those who become disabled are the most expendable workers, and disabled job seekers lose out in competition with others who are sounder in mind or body. The disabled are also affected adversely by any structural changes that reduce the number of unskilled, low-paying jobs to which they are disproportionately relegated.

The Increasing Severity of Disability

Between the 1966 and 1972 surveys of the disabled the number of persons reporting a work disability of any type declined, but the number unable to work regularly or at all increased. Those reporting secondary limitations—persons able to work regularly in the same job but less effectively and women unable to do housework—fell by 2.3 million, of which 1.6 million were men. Apparently, in the recession environment of 1972, workers with slight handicaps were less willing to report them; and many with problems had lost their jobs not as a result of their handicaps, but because of economic conditions.

Between 1966 and 1972 the number of severely and occupationally disabled remained relatively constant, although there were dramatic shifts within this group suggesting a marked decline in the availability of jobs or in the work propensity of those with disabilities. The proportion claiming inability to work regularly or at all rose from 55 to 69 percent (table 6). This increase occurred no matter what the degree of limitation. In 1966, 52 percent of the disabled were unable to work regularly or at all, compared with 70 percent by 1972. There were no compositional changes that would explain this dramatic decline in employability. The proportion of the severely and occupationally disabled who were dependent on the care of others declined from 14 to 11 percent. The proportion of nonmarried family heads among the disabled rose from 17 to 20 percent; this increased share of household heads should have been related to higher income needs and work propensities. The number of whites rose slightly, and the number of nonwhites declined; for both groups the proportion of severely disabled increased. The educational attainment of the disabled improved, which should have reduced rather than increased the chances of severe disability since better education is related to greater labor market success.

Table 6. Changes in Incidence of Disability between 1966 and 1972

Disability status	Thousands of persons		
	1966 (aged 18–64)	1972 (aged 20–64)	1966–72 Change
Total disabled	17,753	15,550	−2,203
Severely disabled	6,100	7,717	+1,617
Occupationally disabled	5.014	3,473	−1,541
Secondary limitations	6,639	4,360	−2,279
Severely and occupationally disabled			
No limitations or minor one	5,253	5,015	− 238
Moderate limitations	2,265	1,930	− 335
Severe limitations or dependency	3,537	4,106	+ 569
Severely disabled			
No limitations or minor one	2,325	2,656	+ 331
Moderate limitations	1,184	1,344	+ 160
Severe limitations or dependency	2,550	3,599	+1,049
Occupationally disabled			
No limitations or minor one	2,923	2,361	− 562
Moderate limitations	1,081	586	− 495
Severe limitations or dependency	987	507	− 480

SOURCE: Social Security Administration, U.S. Department of Health, Education and Welfare, 1966 and 1972 surveys of the disabled, unpublished tabulations.

Declining Employment Opportunities

Changes in the characteristics of the severely and occupationally disabled, then, do not explain the dramatic increase in the proportion of handicapped persons unable to work regularly or at all. What occurred was a rapid decline in employment opportunities. Between the 1966 and 1972 surveys the proportions of the severely and occupationally disabled who were not in the labor force increased while the proportions employed declined (table 7). Over the same period, employment and labor force participation increased noticeably among the nondisabled. If the employment rate among the disabled had increased 6 percentage points as among the nondisabled, rather than falling 4 points, there would have been over 1 million additional severely and occupationally disabled persons working in 1972.

Table 7. Employment Status of Nondisabled and of Severely and
Occupationally Disabled, 1966 and 1972

	1966 (aged 18–64)		1972 (aged 20–64)	
Employment status	Severely and occupationally disabled	Non-disabled	Severely and occupationally disabled	Non-disabled
Total				
Not in labor force	59.7	30.2	63.7	22.5
In labor force	39.9	69.8	36.3	77.2
Employed	35.7	67.8	31.9	73.7
Full time	20.4	58.2	18.0	60.6
Part time	15.3	9.6	13.8	13.1
Unemployed	4.0	2.0	4.3	3.5
Male				
Not in labor force	37.8	6.0	50.0	2.3
In labor force	62.2	94.0	52.0	97.5
Employed	55.5	91.3	49.9	95.0
Full time	39.1	83.7	35.0	84.6
Part time	16.4	7.6	13.9	10.4
Unemployed	5.9	2.7	4.0	2.5

SOURCE: Social Security Administration, U.S. Department of Health, Education and Welfare, 1966 and 1972 surveys of the disabled, unpublished tabulations.

The growth of income support was a major reason for the enormous shifts to nonparticipation in the work force by the disabled. As benefit levels improved during the 1960s, the option of not working became more attractive than the low-wage, menial jobs available to the disabled. There also was increased competition for low-skilled jobs as a flood of women, youth, and illegal immigrants entered the labor market. Moreover, there was a decline in the jobs traditionally held by the disabled. For instance, a disproportionate number are farmers, probably because they can work around their handicaps. The decline of small family farms and the commercialization of farming have curtailed the availability of this option. The proportion of the severely disabled with jobs who were working in agriculture fell from 24 percent in 1966 to 15 percent in 1972; among the occupationally disabled the decline was from 13 to 8 percent. This represented an absolute decline of 272,000 jobs, accounting for almost half of the net national decline in farmworkers over the period.

Data are not available to determine what has happened to the employment status of the disabled as a result of the massive recession in 1974 and 1975, but one indication comes from annual work experience data. The number of persons aged 16 to 64 not in the labor force at all because of illness or disability remained constant at 2.5 million from 1966 to 1968 and then rose to 3.1 million in 1971 after the recession. In 1974 the number jumped to 4.3 million. Even this increase did not reflect the full impact. The disabled were overrepresented among the long-term unemployed relying on unemployment compensation and, by definition, were still in the labor force until exhaustion of benefits. A survey in 1975 found that 21 percent of male exhaustees and 19 percent of females were limited in the kind or amount of work they could perform, double the proportions in the total 1970 adult population. [15]

Almost certainly, the next survey of the disabled will document a very substantial drop in employment over the 1970s. Structural shifts in demand, increased competition from women, youth, and illegal aliens, as well as more attractive and readily available income support options, are critically important factors in assessing vocational rehabilitation prospects and policies.

26

2

The Vocational Rehabilitation System

An Overview

Vocational rehabilitation has developed into a major national social commitment over the last decade. Growth was achieved by the proliferation and expansion of separate and uncoordinated programs, rather than as a result of an overall rehabilitation strategy. Disabled veterans have been provided compensation since the beginning of the Republic, and rehabilitation services were initiated after World War I. The federal/state vocational rehabilitation program also goes back to the 1920s. Administered by states and with substantial federal support, this program serves those whose physical or mental handicaps limit work and who are likely to benefit from the receipt of services. Clients range from the most severely disabled to those with only secondary work limitations. Although the federal/ state vocational rehabilitation program has always included income support recipients among its clients, supplementary efforts were added in 1965 to rehabilitate disability insurance recipients and in 1972 to aid blind and disabled beneficiaries of public assistance. A broad range of employment and training programs was launched in the 1960s to aid the disadvantaged, including a not insignificant number of the disabled. Sheltered workshops are the final major component of the rehabilitation system and provide employment for those who have few options in the competitive labor market, including many of the most disadvantaged participants in the federal/state program. There are other disparate education and training activities that are of less significance, such as rehabilitation for workers' compensation claimants and social services for disabled welfare recipients. Also, there is an increasing federal effort to combat employer discrimination against the disabled, although it is too early to assess the degree of commitment or the likely impact.

There is some logic to this evolving system. Sheltered workshops are the employer of last resort as well as a source of services for those most in need. Rehabilitation of severely disabled income transfer recipients is carried out by the federal/state vocational rehabilitation program on a reimbursable basis. The basic federal/state effort serves a mixture of clients, whereas disabled participants in veterans' and manpower programs tend to have, on the average, less severe socioeconomic and physiological handicaps. There are functional linkages among all these components.

Expansion has been rapid on all fronts in the last decade. In fiscal 1975 rehabilitation programs served 1.8 million persons, nearly triple the figure of a decade earlier (table 8). Expenditures rose over this period from $262 million to $1.7 billion, or 3.7 times after adjusting for cost-of-living increases. During the decade ending in 1975 the federal/state system closed a total of 4 million cases, covering an estimated 3.5 million different persons after adjusting for repeaters. A good guess is that sheltered workshops employed nearly 1 million separate clients during the decade, while manpower and veterans' programs together reached about 500,000 handicapped (not including the substantial number of disabled or injured veterans receiving medical and prosthetic services but no formal training).

Since the disabled may participate in more than one program, these totals exceed the number of individuals served. Services may include inexpensive counseling and placement or extensive medical and vocational treatment. Recipient surveys are one means of assessing the degree of double counting and the extensiveness of services. There are, of course, some biases.

Table 8. Vocational Rehabilitation Activity, Fiscal 1975 and 1965

Activity	Fiscal 1975	Fiscal 1965
	Clients served (thousands)	
Total	1,837	616
Federal/state vocational rehabilitation		
Basic program	1,143	441
Services for disability insurance recipients	76	–
Services for Supplemental Security		
Income beneficiaries	46	–
Veterans' vocational rehabilitation	27	9
Sheltered workshops	410	150
Manpower programs	135	16
	Public expenditures (millions)	
Total	$1,740	$262
Federal/state vocational rehabilitation		
Basic program	869	161
Services for disability insurance recipients	81	–
Services for Supplemental Security		
Income beneficiaries	48	–
Innovation and expenditures	24	21
Veterans' vocational rehabilitation	85*	7*
Sheltered workshops	455	50
Manpower programs	178	23

SOURCES: *Manpower Report of the President,* 1976 and 1966; William H. Button, "Sheltered Workshops in the United States: An Institutional Overview," *Rehabilitation, Sheltered Workshops and the Disadvantaged* (Ithaca, N.Y.: Cornell University, 1970); *State Vocational Rehabilitation Agency Program Data, Fiscal Years 1968 and 1975* (Washington: U.S. Department of Health, Education and Welfare, 1969 and 1976); *Veterans Benefits Under Current Educational Programs* (Washington: Veterans Administration, June 1974); *Caseload Statistics, State Vocational Rehabilitation Agencies, 1974* (Washington: U.S. Department of Health, Education and Welfare, 1975); Sar Levitan and Garth Mangum, *Federal Training and Work Programs in the Sixties* (Ann Arbor: Institute of Labor and Industrial Relations, 1969); *Annual Report, Administration of Veterans Affairs, 1965* (Washington: U.S. Government Printing Office, 1965); Greenleigh Associates, *The Role of Sheltered Workshops in the Rehabilitation of the Severely Handicapped* (New York: Greenleigh Associates, 1976) Vol. II; *Special Analysis J, Budget of the United States Government, 1977* (Washington: U.S. Government Printing Office, January 1976); and Committee on Ways and Means, U.S. House of Representatives, *Committee Staff Report on the Disability Insurance Program* (Washington: U.S. Government Printing Office, July 1974).

* Does not include special benefits for housing adaptations, cars, or special equipment, or for medical or other treatments provided to disabled veterans outside or instead of vocational training; does include estimate of costs for counseling psychologists and vocational rehabilitation specialists employed by the Veterans Administration.

Some clients forget or choose to ignore assistance, especially as the years pass. Others may credit only one agency with providing or delivering services when, in fact, several were involved. Clients may credit success to their own efforts rather than to help they received. Yet recognizing these biases, the views of recipients are useful in discounting inflated program data.

A fourth of disabled persons in 1972 reported having received rehabilitation services, and 36 percent of these received them in the previous year (table 9). The likelihood of participation did not vary with the degree of disability, but disabled males were half again as likely to be served as disabled females. More detailed 1966 data revealed that those under 45 years of age were twice as likely to have been assisted as those who were older. Recipients of income support were served twice as frequently as other disabled persons.

Table 9. Disabled Reporting Having Received Rehabilitation Services, 1966 and 1972

| Disability status | Ever received services | | Received services in previous year | |
	(thousands)	(percentage of all disabled)	(thousands)	(percentage of all disabled)
1966				
Total disabled	2,136	12	694	4
Severely disabled	802	13	319	5
Occupationally disabled	657	13	173	4
Secondary work limitations	677	10	202	3
1972				
Total disabled	3,896	25	1,392	9
Severely disabled	1,914	25	728	9
Occupationally disabled	928	27	305	9
Secondary work limitations	1,054	24	359	8

SOURCE: Social Security Administration, U.S. Department of Health, Education and Welfare, 1966 and 1972 surveys of the disabled, unpublished tabulations.

Private agencies provide most rehabilitation services. Only a seventh of the currently disabled who had received services listed the federal/state vocational rehabilitation program as the provider. One in ten reported direct assistance from the Veterans Administration. Altogether, one-third received services from public agencies. Personal physicians provided services to more than a fifth, and hospitals or rehabilitation centers to more than two-fifths (table 10). The secondary role of public agencies as service providers is perhaps not startling, since they frequently contract with private deliverers rather than provide aid directly. Yet only a third of disabled recipients reported that services were arranged by public agencies. Doctors and the disabled themselves assumed primary responsibility.

Table 10. Reported Sources of Rehabilitation Services Received by Disabled, 1972

| | Percentage of group reporting services* | | |
Source of services	Disabled	Severely disabled	Recovered
Provider of services			
Vocational rehabilitation agency	13.9	10.9	6.6
Veterans Administration	10.2	10.1	11.9
Public welfare	6.2	6.0	0.8
Other public agency	9.1	8.8	7.4
Hospital or rehabilitation center	43.5	47.2	46.8
School	6.8	3.9	5.5
Own doctor	21.0	21.4	26.9
Other private person	5.3	6.2	3.8
Employer (on the job)	6.0	3.5	11.6
Private agency	5.9	6.2	6.8
Not available	1.6	2.5	1.1
Arranger of services			
Vocational rehabilitation agency	10.6	9.4	4.4
Veterans Administration	10.2	10.3	12.7
Public welfare	6.1	5.9	1.1
Other public agency	6.5	7.3	6.6
Own doctor	51.0	55.3	57.0
Other private person	4.3	4.2	1.5
Employer (on the job)	6.7	4.2	10.2
Private agency	2.1	2.3	5.3
Disabled individual	15.1	14.8	18.8
Not available	1.5	0.8	2.2

SOURCE: Social Security Administration, U.S. Department of Health, Education and Welfare, 1972 survey of the disabled, unpublished tabulations.

* Totals may be greater than 100 percent because some recipients report more than one source of services.

Three-fourths of the disabled who had received rehabilitation services felt that the services had helped in some way, such as improving mobility, self-care capacity, self-confidence, or employability. Yet only 11 percent claimed they got a job or a better

31

job as a result, and only 8 percent said they were enabled to do their old job better. Less than one in eight severely disabled recipients felt that rehabilitation had contributed to labor market success.

These data raise some important issues. First, there is a vast disparity between activity levels reported by program officials and by the disabled. Only 1.4 million disabled persons in 1972 and 335,000 recoverees claimed they received services from any source in the previous year. If 11 percent of services were arranged by vocational rehabilitation agencies, 6 percent by public welfare agencies, 10 percent by the Veterans Administration, and 7 percent by other public agencies, an estimated 600,000 persons would have received services arranged by public agencies. Yet, in fiscal 1972 the vocational rehabilitation program alone reported serving 1.1 million cases, while manpower and veterans' programs assisted an estimated 100,000 and sheltered workshops another 300,000. Some clients might not have known which agency arranged their services, or even that any public agency was involved. Forgetfulness is possible, but most people remember significant personal experiences in the past year. Clients might not have credited minimal services, but this would only largely reflect the small impact of such services. Differences of this magnitude are difficult to reconcile.

It is also difficult to reconcile the performance claims of rehabilitation programs with the impact assessments of the disabled. In fiscal 1972 some 300,000 persons were reportedly placed in jobs, not counting placements by the manpower and veterans' programs. Yet only a fourth of the disabled who had ever received rehabilitation services from any source believed that these had improved their status in the labor market. And if this held true for the 600,000 persons receiving services arranged by public agencies in 1971, then the total aided by *all* public programs in improving employability would be only 150,000, or half of the annual number reported successfully placed by the vocational rehabilitation program alone.

These aggregate survey data are not conclusive, but they offer a striking and useful contrast to the more extensive program data that usually serve as the basis for analysis. For instance, program data can leave the impression that public efforts are the major source of rehabilitation services. This is not the case. These survey data, which raise questions about the extent of double-count in the agency-reported data and about the degree to which "meaningful" services are provided, suggest that the claimed impacts on the employability of participants need to be closely examined.

The Foundation: Federal/State Vocational Rehabilitation

The federal/state vocational rehabilitation program is the cornerstone of the vocational rehabilitation system. Founded more than half a century ago, it has experienced rapid growth since the mid-1960s. In fiscal 1965 under the basic grant program, 441,000 cases were served and 135,000 successfully rehabilitated (figure 5). In the next decade the annual caseload grew to 1,143,000, including 306,000 rehabilitated; outlays increased more than fivefold, to $868 million. The federal government contributed the lion's share in the partnership, accounting for 77 percent of funds in fiscal 1975 compared with 62 percent a decade earlier. Adding reimbursed services for public assistance and disability insurance beneficiaries, the total expenditure for federal/state vocational rehabilitation activities in fiscal 1975 was over $1 billion. Despite this rapid growth, however, there has been a basic continuity in administrative approach, client selection, and services. Changes have been evolutionary rather than cataclysmic.

Administrative approach

There are independent vocational rehabilitation agencies in each state that operate a number of local offices. The disabled are referred from a variety of sources; usually each person is assigned immediately to an individual counselor, who collects basic data to determine eligibility. Those who have verified disabilities that are a substantial handicap to employment and who can be expected to improve with help are eligible. Those not accepted may be referred elsewhere, and they may appeal

33

Figure 5. Federal/State Vocational Rehabilitation Programs, Fiscal 1960 to 1975

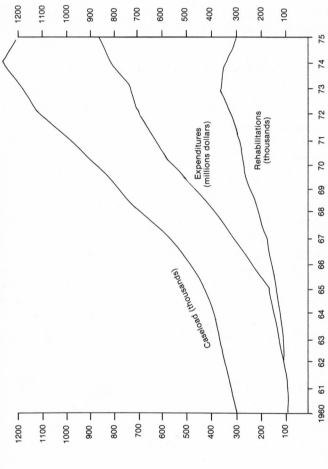

SOURCE: Rehabilitation Services Administration, U.S. Department of Health, Education and Welfare, "Information Memorandum RSA-IM-76-29," mimeo, October 1975.

the decision. When it is uncertain whether the applicant can be helped, he or she may be accepted for evaluation of up to eighteen months, during which time nonvocational services are provided and assessments made. At or before the end of this period, the applicant either is added to the active caseload or is dropped.

Everyone who is accepted joins a counselor in developing a rehabilitation program that outlines goals and needed services. The counselor then arranges for the delivery of services, which may include counseling, physical restoration, training, education, maintenance, work adjustment, placement, help in establishing a small business, social services, or other aid. In theory the resources for any client are unlimited, depending solely on individual needs. The counselor and other rehabilitation agency personnel may deliver the designated services or purchase them from private or public sources. Participants who find a competitive job and hold it for two months, homemakers with improved functional capacity, persons moving into permanent employment in sheltered workshops, unpaid family workers, and the self-employed are counted as rehabilitants. Those who drop out or complete their service program without employment are counted as nonrehabilitants.

Referrals to vocational rehabilitation agencies come from a wide range of sources, and little outreach is involved. Educational institutions account for one in six referrals, hospitals and health organizations one in five, welfare agencies one in ten, correctional institutions and other public organizations one in five. A third of applicants who are eventually rehabilitated are either self-referred or sent by a doctor or other private individual. In fiscal 1975 there were 1.2 million new referrals, of whom 534,000 were accepted, 629,000 rejected, and 42,000 applicants put in extended evaluation.

Client selection

The screening process seems to select the candidates who are potentially most successful, because of either their own perseverance or the predilections of their counselors. In fiscal 1967

35

social security disability insurance recipients, who by definition are severely disabled, represented 26 percent of the nonrehabilitated and 13 percent of the rehabilitated. Their 16-percent share of cases closed in that year was substantially less than their 24-percent share of rejected referrals and applicants. Persons aged 45 and over represented 28 percent of all active cases closed but 35 percent of those not accepted for services.[1]

In fiscal 1970 the ratio of successful to unsuccessful closures was highest for persons having benign neoplasms, hearing problems, visual impairments, and amputations; it was lowest for those with mental illness, conditions of the blood, orthopedic impairments, and mental retardation. Applicant rejection rates averaged a third lower for the high-success-potential groups than for those with more serious handicaps and more limited prospects.[2]

In surveys, counselors indicate that they try to mix their caseloads, balancing some who will require relatively extensive treatment with those potentially needing less assistance. In fiscal 1973, 15 percent of unaccepted closures were persons with handicaps too severe to be served, and 14 percent were those whose problems were judged not severe enough. But among the remainder, such reasons as a client's refusal of services or failure to cooperate may have hidden the counselor bias and self-selection that result in acceptance of those with higher potential.

Creaming is relative, however, and if the vocational rehabilitation program tends to select the disabled with somewhat less serious handicaps and somewhat greater commitment to improvement and recovery, the clients still are seriously disadvantaged. Two percent of rehabilitants are blind in both eyes, an equal proportion are blind in one eye, and the same percentage are deaf. A tenth have impairments of the lower body, and an equal proportion are psychotic or psychoneurotic. One in eight is mentally retarded. Other categories—such as dental problems, hernias, hay fever and asthma, or mild hearing impairments other than deafness—are less severe on the average, but these account for less than a tenth of rehabilitants.[3]

Major Disabling Condition of 1973 Rehabilitants	Percent with Condition
Visual	9
Hearing	5
Orthopedic and amputations	20
Mental illness	31
Mental retardation	12
Respiratory	1
Digestive	7
Heart and circulatory	4
All other	11

Participants also are socioeconomically handicapped. Only a third of rehabilitants in fiscal 1973 were in the prime working years (ages 25 to 44); more than two-fifths were 24 years of age or younger. Nearly a fourth were nonwhite. Only two in five had completed high school, and more than a third had less than nine years of schooling. At referral, 17 percent were working, and a similar percentage listed earnings as their primary source of support. Half relied on family and friends, the remainder on public aid. Some of these clients may have been experiencing only transitional physical or employment problems; overall they may not have been as badly off as the nonrehabilitants, the non-accepted, and the seriously disabled not applying for aid; yet they clearly were a group with serious problems.

Services

The vocational rehabilitation program offers substantial assistance toward overcoming these difficulties. Individual treatment begins with the vocational rehabilitation counselor. In fiscal 1975 outlays for counseling and placement averaged $283 per client served. This included the costs of developing individual plans, arranging services, troubleshooting, and recordkeeping, as well as of job referral and guidance. The adequacy of these services is difficult to judge. According to one comprehensive survey, three-tenths of successful rehabilitants and nearly half of nonrehabilitants were dissatisfied with their

37

rehabilitation plans or claimed that none had been prepared. Less than half remembered receiving any counseling[4] The most recent study of vocational rehabilitation counselor activities, in Florida and West Virginia, found that they spent less than 15 percent of their time in actual counseling; 45 percent was allocated to referrals, eligibility determination, planning, and placement, and the rest to paperwork and other activities.[5] Similar breakdowns have been found in other studies. Placement is not given a high priority in most vocational rehabilitation offices. Only one in five successful rehabilitants in a large follow-up sample claimed to have received help from vocational rehabilitation counselors in finding a job; one in seven had secured a first job after services as a result of this assistance.[6]

Based on the individual rehabilitation plans and with the help of the counselor, each participant is to receive all the individual services he or she needs to realize full vocational potential. In reality, most rehabilitation agencies have a limit on expenditures per client, and clearance is needed when this limit is exceeded. A follow-up of fiscal 1970 rehabilitants by the General Accounting Office found that one in seven felt more services were needed; most frequently mentioned were guidance, counseling, and placement.[7] Moreover, clients requiring expensive services may be weeded out during the referral stage.

Nevertheless, there is no doubt that a broad range of services is available and frequently provided (table 11). Most participants receive diagnostic and evaluation services, which may mean a medical checkup or vocational tests in a sheltered workshop. The most common services are physical or mental restoration and training. Two in five fiscal 1973 rehabilitants had received restoration services. In fiscal 1975, 12 percent of all clients served were provided surgery or treatment, 9 percent prosthetic or orthopedic appliances and 5 percent hospital or convalescent care. The mean cost of hospital care per recipient was $718, the average surgery bill $274, and the price of appliances $220.

Roughly half of fiscal 1973 rehabilitants had received some training. College and vocational school offerings together accounted for roughly half of all trainees. Personal adjustment training (work experience and instruction in self-care) was also important. The value of training is uncertain. Only a fifth of a sample of rehabilitants felt that training had directly helped them in getting a job or that they used training very much in their current job.[8]

Kind of Training	Percentage of 1973 Rehabilitants
Total receiving one or more kinds of training	50.2
College or university	10.4
Elementary or high school	2.7
Business school	3.5
Vocational school	12.3
On-the-job	6.8
Personal and vocational adjustment	21.1
Miscellaneous	10.0

Clients may also receive services from other agencies without the costs showing up in federal/state vocational rehabilitation accounts. A 1965 estimate based on the records of various programs concluded that outside services added 4 percent to the cost of those delivered by the program. A more recent survey found that 23 percent of rehabilitants had been aided during or soon after participation by a welfare agency, 4 percent by the Veterans Administration, 20 percent by private or public employment agencies, and 20 percent by social security agencies. The proportions were even higher among nonrehabilitants.[9] A fuller accounting might include the costs of equal opportunity enforcement, of jobs created under special employment arrangements, of placements into public employment programs, and perhaps even of some costs of job creation for the disabled within the vocational rehabilitation establishment.

With a personalized approach, there is a very wide range in treatment levels. For all rehabilitants the average time from acceptance to closure was 16.4 months in fiscal 1973; the median was 11.6. More than a fifth had been in the program for two years or more, and a third had participated for six months or less. The vocational rehabilitation program spent an average of

$821 to purchase outside services for each 1973 rehabilitant. Yet the outlay was over $3,000 each for 5 percent of rehabilitants; a tenth were provided with no outside services, and another 25 percent received less than $100 worth of purchased assistance. One-fourth of rehabilitants thus received about two-thirds of the outside services purchased by the program.[10]

Table 11. Services Provided by Federal/State Vocational Rehabilitation Program, Fiscal 1975

Kind of service	Percentage receiving service	Average cost per recipient
Diagnostic and evaluation	73	$ 92
Maintenance	20	281
Services to family members	–	128
Other social services	20	141
Postemployment services	–	339
Surgery and treatment	12	274
Prosthetic and orthopedic appliances	9	220
Hospital and convalescent care	5	718
College or university education	11	411
Elementary or high school education	3	233
Business school training	2	422
Vocational school training	7	520
On-the-job training	2	331
Personal and vocational adjustment	8	628

SOURCE: Rehabilitation Services Administration, U.S. Department of Health, Education and Welfare, *State Vocational Rehabilitation Agency Program Data, Fiscal Year 1975*, pp. 16–17.

In fiscal 1975 outlays for the basic federal/state program amounted to $869 million. Reimbursed services for Supplemental Security Income and disability insurance recipients accounted for another $48 million and $77 million respectively; innovation and experimentation expenditures added another $24 million (table 12). Of the total, roughly a fifth went for training and an eighth for physical and mental restoration. Counseling and placement accounted for a third or, combined with diagnostic and evaluation services, for about two-fifths.

Evolutionary changes

Between 1968—when Congress last overhauled the vocational rehabilitation program—and 1975, average expenditures per

Table 12. Vocational Rehabilitation Expenditures, by Service Category, Fiscal 1975

Service category	Total	Expenditures (millions)				Percentage of total expenditures
		Basic vocational rehabilitation	Disability insurance	Supplemental Security Income	Innovation and experimentation	
Total	$1,016.9	$ 868.4	$ 77.3	$ 47.7	$ 23.5	100.0
Counseling and placement	333.7	283.7	28.4	16.6	5.0	32.8
Diagnostic and evaluation	88.9	76.9	6.2	4.9	0.9	8.7
Physical and mental restoration	122.6	104.4	13.1	3.9	1.2	12.0
Training	218.4	187.4	15.9	12.9	2.2	21.4
Maintenance	68.7	65.7	—	2.2	0.8	6.7
Other services	44.8	33.0	7.8	3.6	0.4	4.4
Support of facilities	54.1	43.0	—	—	11.1	5.3
Support of small businesses	10.2	10.2	—	—	—	1.0
Administration	75.5	64.1	5.9	3.6	1.9	7.4

SOURCE: Rehabilitation Services Administration, U.S. Department of Health, Education and Welfare, *State Vocational Rehabilitation Agency Program Data, Fiscal Year 1975*, pp. 1–183.

rehabilitant rose from $1,816 to $2,839, or by 7 percent adjusting for changes in the cost of living. In fiscal 1968, 35.6 percent of funds went for counseling, placement, and administration—the expenses of the vocational rehabilitation establishment. By fiscal 1975 this proportion had risen to 40.2 percent. Meanwhile, restoration and training expenditures dropped from 37.2 to 33.4 percent of outlays. This drop probably reflected a shift toward less costly kinds of restoration services, although the data are not conclusive. The proportion of clients receiving surgery or treatment, which is relatively expensive, dropped from 12.0 to 11.5 percent between 1971 and 1975, and the proportion receiving hospital or convalescent care dropped from 6.2 to 5.2 percent.[11]

There has been increased reliance on sheltered workshops. In fiscal 1965, 46,800 or a tenth of all clients were treated there, and payments to workshops represented a fourth of total expenditures. By 1975 the 223,700 vocational rehabilitation participants treated in workshops accounted for a sixth of the total, and payments represented three-tenths of all expenditures (although both numbers were down from fiscal 1974). The proportion of rehabilitants placed in permanent employment in sheltered workshops rose from 3.2 percent in fiscal 1968 to 3.8 percent in fiscal 1974.

In recent years there have been some important changes in the characteristics of vocational rehabilitation program participants. The mentally ill were 19.6 percent of rehabilitants in fiscal 1968 but 31.4 percent in fiscal 1974; the retarded increased from 10.7 to 12.6 percent. The proportions in other disability categories fell commensurately. For instance, amputees and persons with orthopedic handicaps declined from 24.2 to 19.5 percent of all rehabilitants. Since the mentally ill and retarded tend to be younger than other disabled persons, the median age of rehabilitants dropped from 32 to 28 years between fiscal 1968 and 1974, and the proportion under the age of 25 rose from 26 to 44 percent. Reflecting the expansion of income support, the proportion receiving public assistance rose from 11 to 19 percent over the six years, while the proportion whose primary source of support was earnings fell from 20 to 16 percent.[12]

The Vocational Rehabilitation Act of 1973 mandated increasing services to the more severely handicapped. In fiscal 1974, 114,000 or 32 percent of all rehabilitants were severely disabled according to the definitions developed by the Rehabilitation Services Administration. The number of nonseverely disabled rehabilitants dropped in fiscal 1975, but the severely disabled rose to 116,000, or 36 percent. [13] In the first quarter of fiscal 1976, 38 percent of rehabilitants were severely disabled, as were 41 percent of those newly accepted for services. [14]

Slack labor markets in the 1970s, an expanding caseload, and a more disadvantaged clientele adversely affected placement rates. In 1963, 80 percent of closures were successfully rehabilitated. In 1972, when the national unemployment rate was roughly the same, the success rate had declined to 75 percent. With the severe mid-decade recession, rehabilitations fell to 70 percent of closures in fiscal 1975 as the absolute number of rehabilitations dropped for the first time in two decades. In the first quarter of fiscal 1976 the rehabilitation rate was only 62 percent.

The shift to a more severely disabled clientele after the 1973 legislation was a minor factor in the mid-1970s performance slump. In the first quarter of fiscal 1976 the success rate of the severely disabled was 59 percent, compared with 65 percent of those with less severe problems. This difference, multiplied by the several-percentage-point increase in the proportion of clients severely disabled, could have reduced average success probabilities very little. Over the longer run, however, changes in clientele can be important. The rehabilitation rate in fiscal 1970 of participants with mental illness or mental retardation was 72 percent, compared with 81 percent for all other participants. The increase between 1968 and 1974 in the proportion of clients with a mental affliction could have contributed to a one-percentage-point decline in overall rehabilitation rates.

Performance

Is this complex rehabilitation system effective in achieving its goals of restoring productivity, increasing earnings, and reducing dependency on public transfers? Rehabilitants in 1973 had earned an average of only $14 weekly at referral; four-fifths had no earnings, and those who worked made an average of $72 a week. At closure, 85 percent were receiving wages, averaging $76 weekly for all rehabilitants and $90 for those with earnings. At referral, 17 percent of rehabilitants were receiving public assistance; at closure, only 8 percent. [15]

Although these average gains are substantial, many rehabilitants remain below minimal levels of self-support. In fiscal 1973, 15 percent of rehabilitants had no earnings, 10 percent earned less than $40 weekly, and 28 percent earned between $40 and $80. In other words, less than half of the supposedly successful rehabilitants found jobs in which they earned the equivalent of the full-time minimum wage.

Earnings gains cannot be ascribed to services alone. Clients are selected on the basis of their employment problems, and in any group of unemployed the chances of improvement outweigh the possibilities of deterioration; put another way, the earnings at entry may reflect temporary vicissitudes rather than employment potential. According to one sample of rehabilitants, wages and salaries in the three months before entry were 34 percent above those estimated from referral-week earnings. Those in the previous year were 53 percent higher. [16] A national survey of fiscal 1971 closures found that annual earnings in the calendar year before entry were $1,525 for rehabilitants, double the earnings that would have been realized from 52 weeks of employment at the weekly rate on referral. [17]

Only for those who have suffered from a recent deterioration in physical or mental condition that is likely to be permanent are earnings at referral an accurate indication of future prospects. If disabilities are of longer duration, or if previous earnings are correlated with future success chances, then a longer base period is more appropriate. The choice makes a big difference. For instance, the national survey of 1971 rehabilitants found that annual earnings rose from $1,525 in the prereferral year to $2,225 in 1971, or by 46 percent. Projections from the program data collected at entry and in closure, in contrast, pointed to a gain from $750 to $3,353, a more than fourfold increase.

Not counted in these earnings data are the benefits that accrue to the one in seven rehabilitants who is a homemaker. The economic value of a homemaker's service is difficult to determine. One reasonable valuation of a year's work is around $5,000.[18] Among the two-fifths of disabled women who reported needing household help in 1966, however, three-fourths got it free and the other fourth paid a median of $8 a week, or $416 a year. If vocational rehabilitation services turned those performing no duties into proficient homemakers with a $5,000 output, then this would be a major achievement. If the result were merely to reduce the need for purchasing outside services, the results would be less substantial. According to a 1973 survey of rehabilitants, the percentage reporting currently doing more housework was only 11 percent, barely higher than the 9 percent reporting doing less. Improvements were only slightly higher for persons who had previously been homemakers than for those who had not.[19]

The duration of program impacts is another crucial issue. A person is counted as rehabilitated if he or she is gainfully employed for two months or demonstrates improved homemaking capability. But how long will employment or other improvements continue? A Minnesota follow-up of cases closed to employment between 1964 and 1967 showed that nearly four of five were still working in 1968. A 1970 Wisconsin survey of fiscal 1966 to 1968 rehabilitants found 68 percent employed, and a one-year-after review of fiscal 1968 and 1969 rehabilitants determined that between 65 and 73 percent were still employed. Both a 1974 Michigan study of fiscal 1970 closures and a 1973 sample in California and Pennsylvania found that 57 percent were still working one to three years after rehabilitation.[20] Finally, two-thirds of rehabilitants placed into remunerative positions in fiscal 1970 were still working in 1972, according to a General Accounting Office survey.[21]

Because the vocational rehabilitation system operates as a sorting mechanism, its clients are more likely to succeed than those who are not accepted. Similarly, rehabilitated clients are more advantaged than those who are not rehabilitated. The gains of rehabilitants are not solely the result of services, and comparisons with nonrehabilitants or persons not accepted exaggerate the impact of services.

For instance, a sizable portion of the caseload receives only limited services that are not likely to have a significant impact on long-run employability. One must question whether assistance really "rehabilitated" the one-third of the successes who received purchased services costing less than $100. Although a wheelchair, a cane, or glasses might be sorely needed, many of the clients could afford to purchase such aids if necessary to improve employability. Rehabilitants are in the best position to judge the impact of services. Only 45 percent of rehabilitants in one recent sample felt they had successfully completed rehabilitation. Of those who gave negative assessments, one in three claimed they had received no services, two-fifths did not feel they had completed their plan, and one in ten had completed it but could not find a job. In addition, a fifth continued in the same job, 7 percent sought other means of rehabilitation, and a third stayed home or were unemployed. [22]

How many clients reported as rehabilitated merely moved through the system on paper or received only marginal attention? If only half are given intensive assistance and if the wage gains are realized by those who improve on their own because their problems are less severe, then the effectiveness of services to those most in need may be very much less than the aggregate figures suggest.

With all these caveats, there is little doubt that the federal/state vocational rehabilitation program contributes to the significant improvements in employment and earnings realized by rehabilitants. Some are helped who might make it on their own, and others are given extensive aid despite their limited potential for competitive employment. But the average client has serious work impediments that might not be overcome without some assistance. Rehabilitation methods and priorities may need some adjustment in light of a changing labor market and clientele, but on the average the tried and true approach does produce substantial results.

Without negating the value and overall effectiveness of the vocational rehabilitation program, it is still proper to suggest

THE VOCATIONAL REHABILITATION SYSTEM

that improvements and changes might be made. This cursory review does not provide the basis for detailed policy prescriptions, but it does raise some issues that should be further examined.

Vocational rehabilitation has enjoyed sustained growth. It is difficult, however, to assess the separate impact of each increment in expenditure and of each additional service. An increasing proportion of outlays goes for administration and a declining portion for services. As the shift continues toward serving the most seriously handicapped, placement will lose out as a valid test (and incentive) for program effectiveness. More services will be needed by the more severely disabled, but output will become increasingly difficult to guage, and there will be a consequent loss of accountability. It is vital, then, to determine what is necessary and what is secondary. For example, doubts have been raised about the homemaking component. With no objective standard of successful rehabilitation as a homemaker and no quantification of the benefits, this can, or perhaps has, become a catchall category; the limited evidence indicates that rehabilitation is having little impact on housework capabilities. Another questionable practice is the reimbursed rehabilitation of transfer recipients. The danger is that the rationing methods and treatment strategies that have been developed over the years will become less effective and paperwork will necessarily increase as the sources of funds multiply. Moreover, the inability to reduce welfare caseloads appeciably will reflect negatively on the overall federal/state program.

Perhaps the most important issue is the possibility of marginally declining effectiveness. The recession had a noticeable impact in 1974 and 1975 and, if the 1973 experience is a reliable gauge, improved placement rates should be realized if there is a healthy recovery. Yet, just when changes in the labor market are reducing job opportunities for the severely disabled, the vocational rehabilitation program is giving them increased emphasis, and placement rates are likely to suffer.

There is a need, then, for more careful and critical examination of the vocational rehabilitation program. Control groups are vital for the assessment of long-run impacts on clients. Attention must be given to the implications of serving the more disadvantaged in a slack labor market. Certain aspects should be subjected to careful scrutiny, such as the training of disabled homemakers and the reimbursed rehabilitation of transfer recipients, so that these do not undermine other primary missions. Finally, there is a need to cut down extraneous services and improve efficiency. The value of vocational rehabilitation is undisputed but, because it serves those whose needs are most pressing, the demand for the highest standards of performance should not be relaxed.

Aid for Disabled Veterans

The Veterans Administration (VA) vocational rehabilitation program, though small in comparison with federal/state efforts, is unique in several ways. Giving help to disabled veterans has traditionally been given a high priority because of their service to the country. The law authorizes vocational rehabilitation services to all veterans found in need, defined broadly enough that it includes some persons who would be unlikely to be accepted under the federal/state program. Vocational rehabilitation for veterans concentrates on training, education, and related services. Physical restoration therapy, prosthetics, and other treatments are provided to disabled veterans as part of guaranteed medical services. There is also an extensive effort to develop jobs for veterans in the public and private sectors. Finally, since almost all participants receive veterans' compensation and since these benefits are not reduced as earnings increase, the income support system is more an inducement than an impediment to work and rehabilitation.

Rigorous comparison of federal/state and veterans' vocational rehabilitation is impossible. Veterans are a distinct but heterogeneous group with readjustment problems that compound the effects of disability. The income support and service delivery systems of programs for veterans are very different from those of other programs. A more basic problem is that there have been few attempts to measure the impact of veterans' services. The approaches of federal/state and veterans' vocational rehabilitation can be compared, but their relative effectiveness can not.

Administration

Veterans who receive disability compensation are eligible for rehabilitation, except in a very few cases where there clearly is no need for help. Compensation is awarded for impairments incurred by a serviceman resulting from accident, injury, or disease, whether occurring in peace or wartime. The Veterans Administration rating board, made up of a physician, a lawyer, and an occupational specialist, determines the extent of disability from the schedule for rating disability, which lists specified disabling conditions from 10 to 100 percent based on the estimated effects on a "typical" worker. Compensation levels are set according to the degree of disability, ranging in 1976 from $35 monthly for a disability of 10 percent to $655 for 100 percent. Although the basic notion is to make up for lost earnings, there is no means test, and compensation is paid regardless of income or assets. [23]

In June 1974 there were 2.2 million compensation recipients, 55 percent with a disability of 10 or 20 percent and 6 percent with a rating of 90 percent or more. Most of these were World War II veterans, less than 400,000 from the Vietnam era.[24] Since older veterans may suffer from nonservice disabilities, the number of compensation recipients is less than the number of veterans with disabilities, estimated at 3.1 million among 20- to 64-year-olds in 1972. On the other hand, compensation and consequent rehabilitation benefits may go to some who are not limited in the kind or amount of work they can perform. The 1972 survey of the disabled found only 280,000 Vietnam-era veterans (5 percent of the total) claiming to be disabled.

It is the Vietnam-era veterans who are the primary targets of rehabilitation, since veterans normally are eligible for only nine years after their release from active duty and for four more years if medical problems delay the beginning or completion of training (with further extensions under certain special circumstances). Until 1974 veterans with disability ratings of 30 percent or above were almost automatically entitled to aid, while those with 10- or 20-percent ratings qualified only if they demonstrated serious employment handicaps. A rating of 30 percent can be awarded for flat feet, a trick knee, missing fingers, deafness in one ear, sinus trouble, gall bladder removal, or a number of other conditions that would not necessarily limit job performance. Yet it is recognized that some with lesser disabilities might have greater difficulties on the job considering their individual capabilities and work experience. To reach this group, rehabilitation benefits were extended in 1974 to those with lower disability ratings without demanding proof of substantial impairment of employability.

The Veterans Administration attempts to locate disabled veterans and to encourage them to enroll in vocational rehabilitation as early as possible. Both military and VA hospitals have psychologists available to counsel disabled patients. In addition, counselors from the regional offices visit these hospitals to begin the process of determining an education or training plan for the disabled serviceman or veteran. Those men who are not reached while in the hospital are contacted after applying for disability compensation. When it becomes necessary, the VA can work with state agencies on behalf of veterans who reach the end of their eligibility without completing their rehabilitation, to ensure that the federal/state agencies will continue to aid the victims for the remainder of their program. Other disabled veterans who are not entitled to VA vocational rehabilitation are referred to state agencies from which they can receive assistance.

Services and Costs

The disabled veteran receives medical attention before leaving military service and is eligible for continued care thereafter. The rehabilitation program, therefore, places primary emphasis on training and education. In addition to covering fully the costs of school, apprenticeship, or on-the-job training—including tuition, fees, books, supplies, and equipment—the program offers a subsistence allowance during and for two months after rehabilitation. The allowance is related to family size and kind of training. In 1976 an unmarried veteran in vocational rehabilitation received $201 a month. When combined with compensation benefits, this allowance usually is adequate to maintain the veteran until he can work again. Another option available to disabled veterans is regular GI Bill educational benefits, which were $270 a month for a single person in 1976 but with no stipend for tuition, fees, and other school expenses. Correspondence courses are funded under the GI Bill but not under vocational rehabilitation, and some disabled choose the former for this reason. Before 1974 those with 10- to 20-percent disability rarely qualified for vocational rehabilitation and therefore turned to GI Bill benefits; now they will most likely prefer the more lucrative rehabilitation stipends.

Higher education has become the major emphasis of veterans' rehabilitation. In fiscal 1974, 52 percent of veterans in training were in colleges and 20 percent in junior colleges, as compared with 40 percent in institutions of higher education in fiscal 1967. Vocational and technical training have correspondingly declined from 52 to 21 percent of trainees. It is likely that this trend will continue with the expansion of benefits to persons with 10- and 20-percent disabilities who are likely to be attracted because regular GI Bill benefits do not cover rising college tuition costs.

Special programs have been developed for severely disabled veterans whose handicaps prevent them from beginning an institutional or on-the-job training program. Mobility training and Braille lessons for blind veterans are provided by the VA's Department of Medicine and Surgery, although veterans can also use outside rehabilitation facilities. Remedial education is available for those who need it before entering vocational training. Some disabled veterans requiring a protective setting as a transition into competitive employment are placed in sheltered workshops. None of these kinds of special restorative training is considered a vocational rehabilitation program by itself; rather each is a step toward ensuring that the disabled veteran will successfully complete his training or education and be placed in a permanent job. Another special program is homebound training which is available to severely disabled but intellectually capable veterans who can undertake a training course only in their homes. The aim is usually to develop a skilled trade or profession, such as repair work or accounting, which can be pursued as a small business in the home. These various special efforts are, however, only a small part of the vocational rehabilitation program, serving approximately 800 severely disabled veterans in fiscal 1971, or less than 3 percent of all trainees in that year.

Other forms of readjustment assistance are available to disabled veterans. Under a program established in 1946, veterans receiving compensation for the loss of a hand or foot or for serious impairment of vision are eligible for aid in purchasing an automobile or other conveyance, along with the necessary adaptive equipment. In fiscal 1975, 4,615 vehicles were purchased at an average cost of nearly $3,000, and adaptive equipment was provided for 7,600 vehicles at an average cost of $460. In addition, paraplegic veterans are eligible for assistance in constructing suitable housing, including the special facilities they require. In fiscal 1975 there were 620 such grants averaging over $23,000.

Placement and job development efforts are an important adjunct to training. Veterans employed before entering the services are entitled to regain their previous positions; the disabled who cannot perform in their old jobs are entitled to comparable work. The Office of Veterans Reemployment Rights in the Department of Labor handles complaints and action. Federal and many state and local civil service systems give preference to veterans, especially if they are disabled. The Employment Service also gives them priority in job placement. The Vietnam-Era Veterans Readjustment Assistance Act of 1972 set placement targets, provided for more intensive services, and required all federal contractors to list job openings with local public employment services. By executive order, veterans were given special attention in federal employment and training programs. For instance, initially one-third and later one-half of the positions created under the Emergency Employment Act of 1971 were set aside for veterans. The National Alliance of Businessmen (NAB) worked with the Veterans Administration and the Employment Service to develop jobs for veterans in the private sector.

The total cost of vocational rehabilitation efforts for veterans is not known. Outlays for rehabilitative medical treatment are not separated from regular medical care, and information on the costs incurred to aid veterans in manpower programs is not available. Budgeted program outlays in fiscal 1975 were $73 million for books, tuition, and stipends, exclusive of an estimated $6 million for counseling psychologists and vocational rehabilitation specialists working within the Veterans Administration. This represented an average cost of $3,000 per trainee in fiscal 1975, not including medical or restoration benefits or resources devoted to placement and job development. Another $14 million went for housing adaptations, an equal amount for cars and special conveyances, and another $4 million for adaptive equipment. The total cost, then, of training, medical treatment, and other assistance probably exceeded $5,000 per client in veterans' vocational rehabilitation, compared with the average outlay of $800 under the federal/state program. And since disabled veterans pursuing a higher education may receive aid for several years, the cost per person served is substantially higher.

Characteristics

Large proportions of disabled veterans are attracted by these lucrative benefits. Through fiscal 1974, 15 percent of all disabled Vietnam-era veterans and nearly a third of those with disability ratings of 30 percent or more had received vocational rehabilitation assistance. If GI Bill benefits are also counted, 55 percent of the disabled veterans received such assistance. In fiscal 1975 there were 25,000 trainees in the rehabilitation program, down from a peak of 32,000 in fiscal 1972 but triple the average for the 1960s before the Vietnam build-up. Since rehabilitation is a time-limited readjustment program, the caseload rises in the years following a war and then declines.

The Veterans Administration tries to reach all of the disabled. Through April 1973, 12 percent of Vietnam-era veterans who trained under vocational rehabilitation had a 10- or 20-percent disability; 60 percent had a disability of between 30 and 60 percent, 16 percent between 70 and 90 percent, and 13 percent had a 100-percent disability rating. Put another way, less than 3 percent of veterans with 10- to 20-percent disability were trained, compared with 24 percent of those with 30- to 60-percent disabilities, 31 percent of those with 70- to 90-percent disabilities, and 26 percent of the totally disabled. According to one sample survey, older and nonwhite veterans were less likely to benefit.[25]

Disability rating 30 to 50 percent	Percentage disabled Vietnam-era veterans trained by vocational rehabilitation
Under age 30	39
Age 30–44	35
Age 45 and over	26
Whites, all ages	41
Nonwhites, all ages	34
Disability rating 60 percent or over	
Under age 30	60
Age 30–44	34
Age 45 and over	48
Whites, all ages	61
Nonwhites, all ages	55

Veterans who have been to college but have not yet completed studies for a degree are most likely to avail themselves of aid. College graduates are the least likely to participate in the program, apparently because they have their diplomas and are ready to get on with their careers.[26]

	Percentage enrolling in vocational rehabilitation			
Education before training	Total disabled	30–60% disability	70–90% disability	100% disability
Less than high school	24	33	40	40
High school	17	31	46	46
Some college	28	39	68	61
College	9	22	33	30

Perhaps not surprisingly, it is the less disabled and better educated who are more likely to complete training successfully. The completion rate for a sample of Vietnam-era trainees was 31 percent for those with less than a high school education, compared with 46 percent for those beginning with a high school diploma, 51 percent for persons with some college, and 57 percent for college graduates. Two-thirds of participants with disabilities of 10 to 20 percent completed training, compared with two-fifths of those with 30 to 60 percent, 37 percent of those with 70 to 80 percent, and 29 percent of the totally disabled. If participation rates are weighted by completion rates, the proportion of completers with 10- to 20-percent disability rises to 19 percent and the proportion with 100 percent disability falls to 9 percent. Likewise, those with less than a high school diploma at entry constituted 19 percent of participants but 13 percent of completers, while those with some college were 23 and 27 percent respectively.[27]

Compared with the total disabled population and those helped by the federal/state vocational rehabilitation program, disabled veterans are a relatively advantaged group. Before receiving services, only 19 percent had less than a high school education, while 23 percent had some college. Seven-tenths were between the ages of 25 and 44. Under the federal/state program only 57 percent of fiscal 1973 rehabilitants were males; 39 percent had a high school education or better, and 35 percent were in the prime working years. Less than one-tenth of federal/state vocational rehabilitation clients were prime-age males with a high school education or better, compared with nearly three-fifths of trained disabled veterans.

The Impacts

Offering expensive and extensive services to a relatively employable segment of the disabled population, the Veterans Administration vocational rehabilitation program should be able to report considerable success. Unfortunately, there is very little evidence. A follow-up of Vietnam-era veterans under 30 years of age with 60-percent or higher disability found that, among those who completed postservice training of any sort, the unemployment rate was 13 percent, compared with 22 percent among those not completing. The dropout rate—the percentage of the total group with no job, not looking for work, and not in training or school—was 9 percent in the first case and 14 percent in the second. [28]

Education rather than disability status seemed to have the most effect on employment success. The emphasis on college education was therefore warranted. Unemployment and labor force dropout rates were substantially higher in 1973 for disabled Vietnam-era veterans who had limited education. In fact, college graduates with 60-percent or more disability did better than high school dropouts with ratings of only 10 to 20 percent: sixty-one percent of college-educated severely disabled veterans who worked in 1973 reported an hourly wage above $4, compared with only 39 percent of slightly disabled high school dropouts (figure 6).

Only over the long run can it be determined whether employment differentials will amortize the substantial investment in higher education. The experience of World War II veterans provides some insights. According to regression analysis of 1967 earnings data, the college educated did much better than those with just a high school diploma. Veterans completing college without aid before or after service earned 40 percent more than high school graduates; those attaining their diploma under the GI Bill or the rehabilitation program earned 28 percent more. This suggests either that getting the degree earlier may be beneficial or that those attending college before going in the service were more talented on the average. The estimated rates of return to college education were higher for veterans than for the total population, whether or not the degree was acquired with government support. Significantly, the presence of a disability reduced the earnings of the college-educated veterans by only 5 percent, compared with 30 percent for high school graduates. [29] For the disabled World War II veteran, the sheepskin apparently was the route into white-collar jobs where earnings losses were not as great.

There is no doubt that, if these relationships hold true in the future, placing a priority on higher education is sound policy. Even a sharply declining rate of return to education would not

Figure 6. Employment and Earnings of Disabled Vietnam-era Veterans under Age 30, 1973

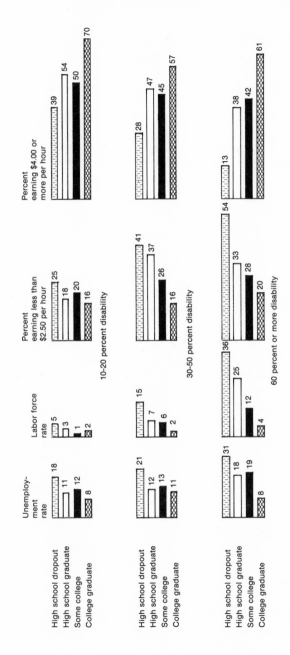

SOURCE: Thurlow R. Wilson, John A. Richards, and Deborah H. Berein, *Disabled Veterans of the Vietnam Era: Employment Problems and Programs* (Alexandria, Va.: Human Resources Research Organization, 1974), pp. 66–70.

make much difference if the disabled college graduate remained so much better off than the nongraduate. It must be remembered, however, that college-educated men were a much more select group in the post-World War II era than they are in the mid-1970s, and that the disabled with college degrees were even fewer in numbers. It is likely that the differentials between those who completed college and those who only completed high school will be less for Vietnam-era veterans than for World War II veterans.

One dimension of the veterans' rehabilitation effort that deserves special attention because it has been tried very little elsewhere is the attempt to change employer attitudes and generate jobs for the disabled. Unquestionably, the greatest success came in the public sector: among severely disabled Vietnam veterans aged 45 years and over in 1973, 45 percent held their longest job in the public sector, as did 30 percent of those aged 30 to 44 years and 20 percent of those under 30 years. In contrast, only a sixth of all workers were employed by the public sector.

In the private sector there was less success. For instance, a combined VA, NAB, and public employment service effort in fiscal 1974 resulted in only 4,800 disabled veteran placements in private business, or less than half the quota, according to NAB data, and probably less in actuality. A fifth of disabled veterans reported that they sought VA assistance in their job search, and more than half used state employment services; but only 2 and 8 percent, respectively, found these the most useful sources of referrals. More than half of those using the public employment service found that their needs for job information and help in contacting employers were not satisfied. Among veterans with 30- to 50-percent disabilities, 35 percent felt they had not been hired because of their disability, as did 51 percent of the severely disabled. High school dropouts were twice as likely to be conscious of discrimination as college graduates.[30] A reasonable interpretation is that job-development efforts worked mostly in the public sector and had their greatest effect in opening doors for the least disadvantaged. It appears to be difficult to coax employers to hire even the most attractive among the severely disabled in a slack labor market.

In summary, veterans' vocational rehabilitation is a special case in which intensive aid is given to a select group qualifying on the basis of service rather than degree of incapacity. Rehabilitation is provided as a right and does not have to be justified in terms of cost-effectiveness. In the absence of follow-up data, judgments about the effectiveness of this vocational rehabilitation "model" must be based on speculation. It is clear, however, that when public concern over costs is minimized, needs for very substantial services will surface, and this suggests that there are basic though hidden constraints on the federal/state vocational rehabilitation program. It would appear that prime-age disabled males can substantially improve their employment status by a college education and that this may be especially important for the disabled. Finally, if job development efforts can help only the most employable among a group that is on the average less disadvantaged than other disabled groups, there must be some doubts whether efforts to change the behavior of employers through exhortation will have a massive impact (although this does not negate the value of such undertakings, since rhetoric is cheap).

Sheltered Workshops for the Severely Handicapped

Competitive employment is a distant and frequently unattainable goal for the disabled with the most severe mental and physical handicaps, and special arrangements are needed if these persons are to work or prepare themselves for entry into the labor market. Sheltered workshops are the primary mechanism for helping the severely disabled. The workshop is a nonprofit operation engaging in productive activities that can use workers who have very limited skills and abilities. Other services also are usually offered in an effort to rehabilitate clients for later entry into competitive employment.

Clientele

An average of 174,000 persons were registered and 140,000 were in daily attendance at 2,800 workshops in 1975. An

59

estimated total of 410,000 disabled persons were served during the year. The number of workshop participants more than doubled between fiscal 1960 and 1970 and doubled again by fiscal 1975.[31]

There is wide variation among workshops. One of every five focuses exclusively on the mentally ill and retarded. Half are work activities centers employing a range of clients, including the mentally ill and retarded who are so competitively disadvantaged that their productivity is negligible. General workshops with a mixed clientele and a somewhat greater focus on productive output account for a fourth of centers. The remainder are centers for the blind. Workshops as a whole average fifty clients in daily attendance. In general workshops, annual terminees represent half of clients served, but in the other kinds of workshops turnover is one-third or less.

Workshops are truly the employers of last resort. Participants differ, but most have limited chances of competitive employment. In 1974 eight in every ten persons in workshops were mentally ill or retarded, and seven in ten had this as their primary disability. Visual impairments accounted for 10 percent of prime disabilities; orthopedic problems, amputation, and cerebral palsy, 8 percent. More than half of sheltered workshop clients were 24 years old or younger. Half had completed less than the eighth grade or had been in special education. Only a fifth of sheltered workshop clients were living alone or with a spouse. Two-fifths had been supported primarily by public transfers and an equal proportion by family or relatives, before entering the workshop. Only one in six had been employed before entry, most as service workers or laborers.[32]

Workshops have always served the severely disabled, but their clientele has recently become even more disadvantaged. In 1967 only 58 percent of the clients in a national sample of workshops were mentally ill or retarded, but the figure was 71 percent in 1974. The percentage of clients having less than a ninth-grade education remained constant despite the increased educational attainment of the population at large and of vocational rehabilitation clients.[33]

Wage Scales and Work

With such severe handicaps, few sheltered workshop clients can perform up to even minimum competitive standards. Workshops are therefore given special treatment under the Fair Labor Standards Act. They may apply for certification as a "regular program," in which case they must pay not less than 50 percent of the minimum wage. Especially handicapped individuals and those participating in evaluation or training programs may be paid lower rates based on their productivity. Workshops may also apply for classification as work activities centers if the average productivity per client is less than $1,225 per year; in this case they are completely exempted from minimum wage requirements. Whenever a subminimum wage is paid to a handicapped worker, however, it must be based on performance relative to that of nonhandicapped workers; if a client's rate of output is half that of the normal industry output and the prevailing wage for a given job is $3.00 an hour, the workshop must pay $1.50. Although wage determinations are rarely exact, nominal enforcement of such requirements probably increases the share of workshop income going to disabled participants but also reduces the competitive advantage that might come from lower labor costs.

Workshops tend to focus on unskilled, labor-intensive work. Packaging and bench assembly account for 10 percent or more of total work in two-thirds of shops. Collating, mail sorting and stuffing, mechanical assembly, woodworking, inspection, and custodial work are also important, each accounting for more than 10 percent of total work in roughly a third of workshops.[34] Manufacturing is the major activity in workshops for the blind. For all workshops it accounted for a fourth of the gross business income in 1971. Salvage, reclamation, and other services accounted for nearly half of 1971 workshop income, 86 percent of this being earned by Goodwill Industries.[35] Subcontract work, though accounting for only a fourth of gross income, is important to many smaller workshops. A third of a sample of workshops in 1974 relied entirely on subcontracts, and another fifth received over 70 percent of their income from such business.[36] One source of subcontracts is the federal government. Under the Wagner-O'Day Act certain goods and services are earmarked for purchase from sheltered workshops. But the 84 workshops benefiting from these provisions in 1974 generated less than 2 percent of total workshop business income.

Workshops vary widely in their business orientation and success. Those for the blind are more business oriented than others. The median business income for blind workshops in 1974 was $250,000, or typically $4,200 per average daily attendee after subtracting direct costs. Work activity centers, in contract, had net income of only $500 per daily participant, and workshops specifically for the mentally ill and retarded netted only $1,300.

With limited business income per worker, wages are necessarily low. The mean hourly wage in workshops for the blind was $1.59 in 1974. In workshops for the mentally ill and retarded, where the mean hourly wage was $0.80, only a fifth earned more than $1.10 . In work activities centers the average hourly wage was $0.46, and 19 in 20 workers earned less than $1.10 an hour. Annual income is reduced by layoffs and short workweeks. The average 1974 annual wage per person in daily attendance was $1,050 for all workshops. Workshops for the blind paid the highest annual wage of $2,610; general workshops were next with $2,010; but those that focused on the mentally ill and retarded averaged only $1,030 and work activities centers only $520.

Finances and Administration

Substantial overhead and administrative expenses are incurred in operating workshop businesses. Yet facilities and staff also deliver services that are not related to production, and it is difficult to separate business from nonbusiness activities. Workshops received an estimated $650 million in business income in 1974. Client wages and other direct expenditures were $405 million; overhead $175 million; and staff, consulting, and wages to nondisabled workers $420 million. According to one estimate 39 percent of staff costs went for general administration, 35 percent for vocational evaluation, training, or placement, 12 percent for work supervision and 14 percent for other services.[37] Thus, between a fifth and a third of staff costs are connected with production. Using the higher figure, staff costs of $140 million might be allocated to production. If facility costs were split evenly between production and service, this would mean that business operations were roughly breaking even.

Whatever the viability of business operations alone, few workshops as presently constituted with their varied service functions are self-sustaining institutions. Business income was supplemented by $280 million in referral income for evaluation, training, and employment in 1974. Public grant programs contributed $175 million, and private charities added another $100 million. The subsidies were sufficient to put workshops as a whole in the black and to allow capital expenditures estimated at $75 million in 1974. But two-fifths of shops have operating deficits in a typical year. The 1974 public subsidies per person in workshops amounted to—

Kind of workshop	Per person served	Per person in daily attendance
Work activities	$1,000	$1,700
Mentally retarded	1,200	2,700
General	1,400	4,100
Blind	2,300	3,700

In 1974 two-thirds of all workshop clients received services paid for directly by the federal/state vocational rehabilitation program and another 7 percent by state agencies for the blind. Employment services included sheltered work, vocational evaluation, training, and placement. Roughly a fourth of workshops received public subsidies to provide jobs.

Evaluation programs ranged from complex psychosocial testing to simple observation and rating of work performance. Almost all workshop clients received work evaluations, and two-thirds were given psychosocial examinations. Training varied from on-the-job assistance in performing assigned tasks to specific occupation-oriented training. Eighty percent of clients received help in adjusting to their jobs, and seven in ten received vocational guidance, but less than half received occupation-related training. Placement services were offered, but they were not a major component of most programs: three-fifths of workshops reported spending less than $500 annually on professional staff for placement. One-third of all workshops, including 44 percent of work activities centers, either had no placement functions or did not achieve any competitive placements in 1974.[38]

The Benefits of Work and Services

The goal of vocational services is placement into competitive employment. One-sixth of clients had been working before entry into the workshops. Seven of ten in the workshop felt they were ready for competitive employment, and the same proportion felt they would be placed in the near future. Yet only about one client in ten was placed in 1974, representing half of all terminees. There was no correlation between services and placement, except that job-readiness training usually preceded placement. High vocational capability at entry, and less severe disabilities were the major determinants of placement success. It is estimated that more than one in seven terminees are subsequently readmitted, suggesting that many fail after a period in competitive employment. Furthermore, it has been asserted by some that workshops tend to discourage mobility of their most productive employees in order to meet production quotas.[39]

Many nonvocational services are offered in sheltered workshops. Roughly two-fifths of all shops provide assistance in developing skills of independent living, such as personal hygiene. A fifth offer speech therapy, a similar proportion homemaker training. A third of units for the blind have training in mobility and communication. About half of all workshops offer recreation and social programs, social services, and remedial education. Psychotherapy, homebound employment, transportation, housing, and other services are provided less frequently. In addition, roughly a third of workshops provide psychological and medical examinations; about one in ten provides physical restoration or aids to the blind. The proportions of all participants actually receiving such services are, of course, very much smaller.

Without minimizing the value to those served, it must be recognized that the impact of services on the entire workshop population is small. Eleven percent in one large sample of clients moved into independent residential status between entry and termination, but 6 percent moved into dependency. The net percentages improving in dressing, food preparation, personal hygiene, mobility, or activity limitation ranged from zero to 2 percent.[40]

The overall effectiveness of sheltered workshops is difficult to determine. It is hard to be unemotional about an institution that provides the only productive activity and an important income supplement for such an unfortunate group. It is also difficult to separate service from employment inputs and outputs. Despite extensive recent investigation, however, important questions remain unanswered.

There is no doubt that when workshops are self-supporting, or almost so, and when they employ those who would otherwise be idle, they are worthwhile. Even if businesses operate at a loss, public subsidies are warranted because otherwise income transfers would probably be needed for the clients. But if public costs exceed wages severalfold, the therapeutic benefits of work and services must be proved.

Some of the funds for manpower services are probably a hidden subsidy for sheltered employment. But the lion's share goes for staff and related overhead. Public resources have been tied to the provision of rehabilitation services, and it is through public subsidies that workshops have thrived. Despite the attention given to evaluating vocational potential, training, placement, and other services ostensibly directed toward securing competitive employment, the share of workshop clients moving on to jobs in the competitive sector differs little from the share employed at entry. Some have concluded from the poor placement record that vocational rehabilitation must be given even higher priority in workshops. An alternate conclusion is that the services currently provided are not especially effective in increasing employability, probably because the goal of competitive employment is unrealistic for most workshop clients. The value of other services is more difficult to assess, since they are usually not associated with quantifiable objectives. It remains unclear whether workshops are the best delivery mechanism, whether the services are really needed, and whether clients benefit in proportion to costs. The evidence that only a very small minority of them show any tangible improvement raises the question of whether all would not be better off with wage subsidies equal to the cost of services.

In the end, the effectiveness of workshops depends on their ability to provide work and wages. Their business viability is therefore the crucial question. Sheltered workshops grew steadily over the last decade, despite the structural changes in the economy that left the severely disabled further and further behind competitive employment standards and despite dreary business conditions. The workshops expanded by rapidly increasing nonbusiness revenues, emphasizing rehabilitation services rather than employment, and lowering relative wages paid to disabled employees.

The minimum wage regulations applied to sheltered workshops are intended to protect the disabled against exploitation, not to raise their wage floor. In 1967 total client wages divided by average daily attendance equaled $1,293. By 1974 the average annual wages had declined to $1,080, or by two-fifths in real terms. The figures are not strictly comparable, of course, but changes of this magnitude are not statistical flukes. Over the same period there was a substantial shift in emphasis from earning business income to delivering services. Business income accounted for four-fifths of all workshop revenues in 1967 but for only 54 percent by 1974. Staff costs rose from roughly one-fifth to two-fifths of expenditures, while client wages fell from more than one-third to less than one-fifth.[41]

Income	Percentage of total	
	1967	1974
Business	79	54
Referral	8	23
Community	8	8
Other	5	15
Expenditures		
Staff	22	39
Client wages	35	17
Materials and supplies	24	21
Overhead	19	23

As a consequence, there were some rather staggering changes in performance measures. Average expenditures per client-year rose from $3,700 to $7,100 between 1967 and 1974, while the public cost (charity plus government contributions) tripled to $2,500, and the average public cost per placement tripled to $6,500.

The evolution of workshops into more comprehensive rehabilitation centers placing less emphasis on productive employment may or may not be a salutary development, but it certainly raises some serious questions. For instance, if it costs $1 in overhead and expenses to generate $2 in earnings and productive labor, the expenditure would be worthwhile. If organization and service costs are $2 or slightly above for each $2 earned, work might still be preferred over transfers because of rehabilitative impacts and contributions to the self-esteem of clients. But the average aggregate expense for every dollar of client wages rose from $2 to $6 between 1967 and 1974. To the extent that this rise represented an increase in services, other benefits should have been realized, such as greater vocational improvement for clients. Placement rates declined from 17 to 13 percent of those served between 1967 and 1974. Though reflecting both a more disadvantaged clientele and changed economic conditions, these results do not show that increased services have substantially raised employability. Given the lack

67

of evidence that services have considerable payoffs, it seems questionable to be paying more than $2 in staff costs for each $1 in client wages. Sheltered workshop administrations can not ignore the charge that employment programs designed for the disabled have apparently become employment programs for the social service workers.

Workshops have expanded essentially because large segments of those being treated by vocational rehabilitation can not be placed in competitive employment or require long and expensive treatment first. It will be necessary to expand workshops if the severely disabled are to be helped, as is planned. In fact, workshops must grow even if vocational rehabilitation's severely disadvantaged caseload remains constant; the typical participant stays more than a year, and thus fewer and fewer new positions open up without growth. Yet the capacity of the sheltered workshop system to expand continuously and effectively is questionable. Economies might be realized by cutting marginal services, but business or wage subsidies will probably be needed for expansion. Such a step is unavoidable if the more seriously handicapped are to become the major target of public rehabilitation efforts.

3

The Underlying Issues

The Universe of Need

Vocational rehabilitation efforts seek to increase the employability of those who are limited by mental or physical handicaps, but not all disabled are feasible candidates. It is useful, therefore, to estimate the number of persons with serious needs who want and could benefit from rehabilitation services.

This is not a simple procedure. By definition, the disabled are limited in the kind or amount of work they can do. But some may have perfectly adequate earnings; others without earnings may be receiving income transfers; still others may have so little vocational potential that services could do little to enhance their employability. Any reasonable estimate of needs must screen out persons with less consequential difficulties, as well as those with problems so severe that they can never be overcome and those who do not want help. There are no hard-and-fast rules. Some might consider anyone with a secondary work limitation to be outside the universe of need even if unemployed, while others might consider a severely disabled person a candidate for services even if fully employed. The functionally dependent might be included in the target population by those who believe that anyone can and should be helped no matter what the cost, while others might feel that rehabilitation for these persons is not reasonable. Estimates might include anyone lacking successful employment, only those claiming to want jobs or, more narrowly, just those actively seeking work or services.

Any needs estimate, thus, rests on a set of assumptions. Advocates of expanded services, who want to demonstrate unfilled needs, understandably utilize the assumptions that yield the largest estimates. Since vocational rehabilitation has enjoyed widespread support and since most analysis has been done by insiders, the prevailing estimates of need are probably on the high side.

Needs Estimates

The five major universe-of-need studies have yielded estimates ranging from 3.5 to 7.1 million for fiscal 1973.[1] Based on a review of state plans, Harbridge House estimated that 3.43 percent of the population was handicapped and could benefit from vocational rehabilitation services. This would have meant a universe of 5.1 million. At the opposite end of the spectrum an estimate by Nagi—which included all persons under 65 who had retired or left their last employment because of disability, were forced into part-time work, or could not perform housework or schoolwork—yielded the 7.1 million estimate. More detailed calculations by Ridge, by Worrall and Schoon, and by Berkowitz, included the disabled unemployed, "discouraged workers" who were not actively seeking jobs but would work if they had the opportunity, the underemployed, and homemakers with limited capability. The tallies were as follows:

1. The unemployed were estimated by adjusting 1966 unemployment and labor force participation rates for the disabled proportionately with national rates. The 1973 estimated unemployment rate among the disabled was 8.9 percent, the labor force participation rate 53.5 percent, and the projected disabled population was 20.6 million, yielding a tally of nearly 1.0 million unemployed disabled persons.
2. The estimated total outside the labor force desiring work was based on Bureau of Labor Statistics figures giving the number of

persons claiming to want a job but to be not looking because of illness or disability. From this it was projected that 15 percent, or 1.4 million, of the disabled who were not in the labor force desired a job.

3. It was then estimated arbitrarily that 10 percent of the employed disabled could have their skills upgraded by the vocational rehabilitation program, yielding 1.0 million underemployed.

4. The estimates assumed that 30 percent of the disabled homemakers could be helped substantially through vocational rehabilitation services. In 1973 there were 2.0 million who could presumably benefit, or 1.7 million when the double count under the "discouraged worker" category is taken into consideration.

The total universe of need under this procedure would be 5.1 million. If persons with secondary work limitations (able to work regularly in the same job) were excluded on the assumption that their needs were not severe, this would subtract 299,000 unemployed, 300,000 discouraged workers, 556,000 underemployed, and 472,000 homemakers, reducing the target population to 3.5 million.

The universe of need was, then, somewhere between 3.5 and 5.1 million in fiscal 1973 according to these estimates. If vocational rehabilitation caseloads are compared to these figures, as they have been by advocates of expanded aid, there would appear to be major deficits in services. The vocational rehabilitation program served between 23 and 34 percent of the target population in fiscal 1973, depending on which estimate is used; it accepted somewhere between 10 and 14 percent and successfully rehabilitated between 7 and 10 percent.

Reducing Needs Definitionally

Yet, under equally or even more reasonable assumptions, the estimated universe of need is reduced substantially and the service deficit lowered correspondingly.

1. The procedure of counting homemakers is questionable. Although they are eligible for vocational rehabilitation services, there is no standard for determining who needs aid or what the benefits and costs may be. The considerations in dealing with

homemakers are certainly different than in aiding labor force participants. It might be more appropriate, then, to consider two universes of need relative to services. Excluding homemakers from the above estimates, there were 3.4 million disabled persons in need of employment-related services counting those with secondary work limitations, or 3.0 million excluding them. To get a comparable figure for vocational rehabilitation services, those who receive homemaker training should be subtracted. Among the fiscal 1974 rehabilitants, one in seven were homemakers. If six-sevenths of the vocational rehabilitation clients are assumed to receive employability services, this represents between 30 and 34 percent of the estimated universe in need of such services. Rehabilitants securing jobs represented between 9 and 10 percent.

2. The estimates of unemployment are lower if based on 1972 survey data. In that year only 710,000 disabled were jobless, or 485,000 excluding those with secondary work limitations, compared with the estimated 979,000 and 680,000 projected for 1973 from 1966 data.

3. The estimate of 1.4 million disabled in 1973 not in the labor force but wanting a job is certainly suspect. While 12 percent of those not in the labor force because of illness or disability claimed they currently wanted a job, many of the disabled who were not in the labor force apparently did not think their disability was the reason for their not seeking work. There were only 619,000 persons in 1973 who claimed they wanted a job currently but were not looking because of illness or disability, and some of these were merely ill rather than disabled. Furthermore, subjective responses to questions of job desire are difficult to interpret. Many of the disabled may want a job but are unable to work because they are too incapacitated. Others may claim—because it is socially acceptable—to want a job but really have little desire. As noted previously, the overwhelming majority of the disabled who quit working after onset did so under doctor's order or because of their own desire to quit and not because they believed jobs were unavailable. Assuming arbitrarily that half of the 619,000 are disabled, desire employment, and can feasibly work with assistance, the universe of need would be 310,000, including 60,000 persons with secondary work limitations.

4. The estimate of 1.0 million underemployed disabled workers is probably understated. The 1972 survey found that, among the 6.7

million employed disabled, 18 percent earned under $50 a week (compared with 0.7 percent of nondisabled workers but also a fifth of federal/state vocational rehabilitants placed in paying jobs in that year). This estimate of the underemployed would yield 1,179,000 persons in 1972, including 259,000 persons with secondary work limitations.

Using these alternative figures (and assuming they held true for 1973, when economic conditions improved), the universe of need would be 2.2 million, or 1.7 million excluding those with secondary work limitations.

Any realistic projections would also have to consider the attitudes of the disabled toward rehabilitation. In 1972, 3.2 million disabled persons were interested in receiving some services, or 2.4 million excluding persons with secondary work limitations. Not all of these, however, would benefit from or could be considered in need of services. More than a third of those with an interest were persons who had already received aid. An estimated two-fifths (according to the more detailed 1966 data) were already employed, and half had an income above the poverty level, as did 22 and 40 percent, respectively, of the severely disabled with an interest in services. Between 1966 and 1972 the proportion of the disabled receiving services apparently increased dramatically, but so did the proportion still interested. Interest is probably related to availability. If 25 percent of those wanting services are assumed not to have severe needs, realistic prospects, or a real commitment, then the universe estimates would range from 1.8 to 2.4 million.

Comparing vocational rehabilitation totals with these figures exaggerates the service deficit in two ways: First, the vocational rehabilitation program is only one possible service deliverer. If there is a deficit, it may make sense to expand the vocational rehabilitation program, but the deficit must be calculated by considering *all* providers. As noted, more services are arranged by private than by public sources, of which the federal/state vocational rehabilitation program is only one. Second, the ratio of services to needs compares a flow with a stock, namely, persons served each year with all disabled persons in need of services.

It is difficult to estimate the annual number of persons who either become disabled and need services or have a deterioration in conditions generating need. The Rehabilitation Services Administration has estimated that there were 801,000 new potential clients in 1972 and projects that the figure will rise to 867,000 by 1977. Another study based on state plans came up with a figure of 912,000 annually.[2]

The basis for these estimates is unclear, but they appear to be on the high side. A 1971 survey of recently disabled adults found that 1.7 million persons became disabled between October 1969 and March 1971. On an annual basis this amounted to 1.2 million, including 574,000 severely disabled, 245,000 occupationally disabled, and 339,000 with secondary work limitations. Yet in 1971 more than a fourth of the newly disabled were employed full time, compared with half the nation's work force.[3] If the differential is used as an estimate of the extra need generated by disability, this would mean that only 280,000 persons with serious labor market problems are added annually to the disabled.

Additional increments in need are generated when those already disabled suffer physical or economic setbacks. Among the 2.3 million disabled persons employed full time in 1966, some 573,000 either were not in the labor force, were unemployed, or were employed part time three years later. If half of these are arbitrarily and conservatively assumed to be in need of services (some may choose to work part time, and most of those outside the labor force do not want jobs), the number coming into need over three years is 286,000, of whom a third may be assumed to enter the universe of need in any particular year. Adding the newly disabled and those with deteriorating conditions would suggest an annual flow of about 400,000 into the universe of need.

Measured against this total the state/federal vocational rehabilitation program alone is exceeding the annual need and thus cutting into the stock of disabled. Certainly this is the case if all rehabilitation services from all private and public deliverers are counted.

These crude estimates suggest some important considerations in weighing the adequacy of resources. Whereas prevailing universe-of-need estimates have indicated large service deficits, different assumptions yield much lower need totals and raise a new set of policy considerations. It is one thing to help a few of those at the end of the labor queue to move forward into the ranks of the employed; it is another thing to try to reorder rankings entirely. Rehabilitants may have to compete among themselves for a limited number of jobs available to the disabled when the number of such jobs does not grow faster than the number served. Macroeconomic conditions have less impact on selective attempts to place a few workers than on efforts to move an entire cohort into jobs. Displacement on the supply side is also an issue. As the universe of need is increasingly served, the expansion of public programs will substitute for private efforts, and the resulting changes will have more effect on who pays than on the level of services. When subsidized services become more readily available, clients will demand or desire more, even if the increments to their well-being become smaller. As the level of services increases relative to need, it is more and more crucial to consider whether the next increment in services is having the desired effects or an acceptable rate of return. Because an undertaking is worthwhile on the average does not mean that it is worthwhile at the margin, that is, that expansion is warranted. The possibility that vocational rehabilitation services already meet a substantial portion of need makes it critically important to look at the margin. Is there a declining rate of return? Are expanded efforts feasible in a slack labor market? Can the universe of need be reasonably extended to include the more difficult to serve?

The Return on the Vocational Rehabilitation Investment

Central to vocational rehabilitation and manpower programs for the disadvantaged is the notion that public investments in human capital can be profitable. Just as business investments are made on the basis of estimated rates of return, so too, in theory, can decisions about human capital expenditures. Services raise productivity and future earnings, and the present value of this stream of benefits can be compared with program outlays to calculate a rate of return. A benefit-to-cost ratio of 1.0:1 means that the services pay for themselves through the subsequent gains of the recipients. A ratio of 1.2:1 means that the return on the investment is 20 percent, which compares favorably to the payoff sought in business investments.

A number of benefit/cost studies in the 1960s purported to demonstrate the effectiveness of manpower programs for the disadvantaged. These varied in their scope, focus, technical sophistication, and assumptions; some used control groups, others did not; but the results were generally favorable, most frequently yielding benefit/cost ratios between 1:1 and 4:1 under standard assumptions. [4] In the early 1970s these studies were challenged on several counts. Control groups were claimed to be poorly structured. Evidence from longitudinal surveys showed diminishing returns over time and, since a frequent assumption was that gains would last at least ten years, critics claimed that benefit/cost ratios were inflated. Their criticisms not only undermined the belief that manpower programs had succeeded but even led some to conclude that the programs had failed.

In contrast, benefit/cost analyses of vocational rehabilitation yielded payoff rates so high that few questioned the profitability and value of these efforts. The major studies followed a standard format. The earnings before the program were compared with earnings subsequent to completion of rehabilitation. Base-period earnings could include those in the week before entry, those in the quarter before, or those in the preceding year. Because the client may have been recently disabled, in which case the preceding year's earnings would not fully reflect present limitations, most studies used the entry status as a base. Gains were projected under various assumptions. Some studies assumed that earnings at closure would continue to rise in real terms with general productivity increases; other studies did not. Various discount rates were used for estimating the present value of future benefits. The likelihood of future job loss was considered, based on some follow-ups of rehabilitants, the typical assumption being that 15 percent of rehabilitants would lose their jobs in the first year and an additional 5 percent in the next four. (Surprisingly, the probability that certain handicaps would become more severe and affect future work was usually ignored.) Some studies attempted to estimate benefits to homemakers, and others included welfare savings. On the cost side there were a variety of adjustments— deducting income maintenance costs, adding services delivered by other agencies, adjusting for earnings foregone during participation in rehabilitation, and recognizing that some clients would return for more services.

Benefit/Cost Studies

Despite a range of assumptions within this general frame- work, the major studies of vocational rehabilitation pointed to consistently high rates of return. A 1965 study by Ronald Conley utilizing national data for 1959 through 1963 found that, at a 4-percent discount rate, the benefits were fourteen to seventeen times the costs. Under an 8-percent discount rate, the benefit/ cost ratios were between 10:1 and 12:1. In a 1969 update using national program data for 1958 to 1967, Conley found that the ratios ranged from a high of 19:1 in 1958, using a 4-percent dis- count rate and estimating benefits based on earnings at entry, to a low of 3:1 in 1967, using full-year preentry earnings as a base and discounting at 8 percent. Based on 1966 national data, the Rehabilitation Services Administration estimated that each $1 spent on vocational rehabilitation returned $36 in benefits, including the projected value of improved homemaking. Two studies by the Michigan Department of Education using state data for 1968 and 1969 estimated benefit/cost ratios of 33:1 and 26:1, respectively, for these years. An analysis of 1969 Florida data by Donald Bellante calculated benefit/cost ratios for a number of different groups; the highest was 86:1 for nonwhite males with at least twelve years of education who were under 25 years of age and suffered visual disability; the lowest was 2:1

for nonwhite females aged 55 and over who suffered amputations. Similarly, an analysis of a number of special rehabilitation projects by Grigg, Holtmann, and Martin computed ratios ranging from 8:1 to 70:1 for different groups; Wright and Reagles found a range between 74:1 and 17:1 in assessing a 1971 experimental project in Wisconsin. [5]

More recent studies have displayed greater sophistication in their assumptions and techniques, but the results have been equally positive. An analysis of 1970 national data for a number of groups by Monroe Berkowitz yielded a few cases of returns below 1:1, under the most conservative assumptions, but the overwhelming majority of benefit/cost ratios exceeded 10:1 [6] A study by Collignon and Dodson estimated a fourteenfold return in fiscal 1972. [7] Abt Associates computed benefit/cost ratios for the program in fiscal 1970 which ranged from 7:1 to 10:1 under the most conservative assumptions. [8]

The Importance of Methodology

These benefit/cost estimates for vocational rehabilitation exceeded all but the highest estimates for manpower programs. However, the methodologies used differed significantly. Manpower program studies frequently compared enrolees with others who had similar characteristics, whereas none of the major vocational rehabilitation studies included control groups. Manpower program studies also tended to use more conservative assumptions in projecting benefits. The differences can best be illustrated by applying both the manpower and vocational rehabilitation benefit/cost approaches to the same data. One of the most comprehensive, if not the most technically sophisticated, analyses of any training program was a tracking by Department of Labor analysts of the earnings records of 55,000 persons enrolled in 1964 under the Manpower Development and Training Act (MDTA). The Department of Labor studied trainees' earnings from 1958 to 1962 and from 1965 to 1969, using social security records. [9] A control group was selected from other records and matched according to age, race, sex, prior earnings, and prior earnings patterns. Since the social security records did not contain information on education, family status, or a number of other pertinent variables, the control group tended to be less disadvantaged than the trainees, which resulted in an understatement of training's impact, but the basic data can be used to demonstrate the implications of alternate methodologies.

Comparing the absolute income gains of trainees and controls, training seemed to have little impact. Between 1962 and 1965, the full calendar years before and after participation, enrollees increased their earnings by $58 more than controls (table 13). Thereafter, earnings of controls advanced more rapidly, so that the 1962-to-1969 gain for trainees was $61 less than that for the matched group. Even under the liberal assumption that the first-year $58 differential in favor of trainees would continue for five years, the total gain at 6.5 percent discount rate would amount to $257, compared with costs per enrollee of $1,665, yielding a benefit/cost ratio of only 0.15:1.

Since the control group started with higher average earnings, similar gain rates would lead to widening differentials in favor of controls. Comparing rates of gain rather than absolute differentials, therefore, yields a somewhat more favorable picture. Between 1962 and 1965 the earnings of controls rose 75 percent while those of trainees showed a 90-percent rise. If there had been no differential, trainees would have earned $174 less in 1965 than they actually earned. Likewise, if trainees' earnings had grown at the 176-percent rate of controls' earnings rather than 196-percent rate achieved between 1962 and 1969, trainees' earnings would have been $227 less in 1969 than they were. Assuming a twenty-year future work life and a 6.5 percent discount rate, the benefit/cost ratio would be 2:1. Whether this ratio is more appropriate than the smaller one calculated above is debatable, but these figures do suggest the range of assumptions usually applied in manpower benefit/cost studies.

The picture changes rather markedly when vocational rehabilitation benefit/cost methodologies are used. As noted, vocational rehabilitation studies focus on before-and-after changes in the earnings of completers. If this approach is applied to the manpower training data, the programs take on the appearance of spectacular success. Between 1962 and 1965 the average

Table 13. Average Annual Earnings of 1964 Manpower Development and Training Act Enrollees and Controls, 1962 to 1969

	Earnings			1962–65 change		1962–69 change	
	1962	*1965*	*1969*	*Amount*	*Percent*	*Amount*	*Percent*
All enrollees	$1160	$2204	$3429	$1044	90	$2269	196
All controls	1321	2307	3651	986	75	2330	176
Completers	1200	2325	3527	1125	94	2327	194
Completers controls	1368	2331	3657	963	70	2289	167

SOURCE: Employment and Training Administration, U.S. Department of Labor, unpublished data.

earnings of completers rose $1,125. They then increased $710 in real terms by 1969, or roughly 7 percent annually. Assuming, again, discount and real growth rates of 6.5 percent, as well as a twenty-year work life, the current value of the future gains would be $22,500. Divided by the $2,500 cost per completer, this would yield a benefit/cost ratio of 9:1, or more than four times as high as the more liberal ratio calculated using control groups. If the earnings of the preentry quarter are used as the base, rather than earnings of the preceding calendar year, the gain is even greater because many become unemployed during the last quarter. The benefit/cost ratio would then be an estimated 13.6:1 based on last quarter's earnings, or 16.4:1 if based on the status during the week before entry.

Although the assumptions are simplistic, the exercise illustrates the implications of the differing approaches used in calculating benefit/cost ratios. Differences in assessment methodologies, rather than in performance, may account for the much more positive judgments of vocational rehabilitation than of manpower programs.

Questions and Uncertainties

This conclusion would not hold true if the status of the disabled could not be expected to improve without the receipt of services. If this were the case, base-period earnings would indeed be predictive. However, among any group of handicapped persons with employment problems some will recover, some will adjust, and some will get whatever assistance they need on their own. The extent of improvements will depend, not just on services, but on the characteristics of the persons involved. For instance, the 1969 follow-up of persons disabled less than ten years and not in the labor force in 1966 revealed that one in eight was employed in 1969. A fourth of all those under age 45 found employment; the proportion was two-fifths among males this age. Over half of those with some college education improved their disability status or recovered between 1966 and 1969, twice the proportion improving among those with less than an eighth-grade education. More than half of all disabled persons working before onset of disability were employed in 1966, compared with less than two-fifths of those not previously employed.

Relative to their proportion in the disabled universe, prime-age males with previous work experience and a high school education are overrepresented among persons receiving vocational rehabilitation. Thus, the types of persons served are likely to have better chances of recovery and improved employment than others among the disabled. Rehabilitation services can not be credited, therefore, with all the improvements realized by rehabilitants. Only 17 percent of the 1972 disabled who had previously received rehabilitation services felt that the services had improved their employment status. One follow-up study of vocational rehabilitants found only 57 percent crediting the program with any contribution. Another study reported that one in eight rehabilitants did not receive any services, and that many more might have been expected to recover on their own.

The long-run impact of services cannot be determined just from future changes in the employment status of recipients. As the manpower training data suggest, there might be an initial improvement followed by a decline for trainees, compared with a steady increase for controls. According to a vocational rehabilitation follow-up study covering 1971 closures, the change in earnings from the preentry to postclosure years was an increase of 48 percent for rehabilitants, compared with decreases of 19 percent for nonrehabilitants and 28 percent for persons not accepted. Between the first and second years after closure, annual income for the rehabilitants rose only 8 percent, compared with 23 percent for the other two groups.[10]

Liberal projection techniques frequently inflate benefit/cost ratios of the vocational rehabilitation program. For instance, the financing of services from the disability insurance trust fund is based on the notion that the savings resulting from possible benefit terminations will more than equal the costs of services. From 1966 through 1973, 13,000 recipients of reimbursed services had left the rolls. The value of cumulative expenditures was estimated to be $127 million, compared with $317 million in potential transfer savings assuming that those who had become self-supporting would continue to be so. The benefit/cost ratio was, thus, a respectable 2.5:1 for service expenditures in the fiscal 1966–73 period.[11] Based on such promising findings, the percentage of trust funds set aside for financing rehabilitation services was increased in fiscal 1973 and 1974. Yet in the deteriorating economy there was a substantial decline in performance during the 1970s. Using standard assumptions, the ratio of annual savings to expenditures declined steadily from 3.8:1 in 1968 to 1.7:1 in 1973.[12] Expansion had been based on the 2.5:1 ratio of savings to expenditures from 1966 to 1973, but the positive impact had eroded by the end of the seven-year period. More critically, the assumptions used to estimate these returns were invalidated as performance declined. In fiscal 1974, 2,200 beneficiaries who were removed from disability insurance rolls reclaimed their eligibility; their numbers exceeded the total who had returned to social security rolls between fiscal 1966 and 1973.[13] More persons recidivated than terminated in fiscal 1974, and the number currently terminated declined from 12,991 in 1973 to 11,796 in 1974, suggesting negative marginal returns on the $56 million fiscal 1974 outlays. Earlier assumptions that those removed from the rolls would remain self-supporting were clearly invalidated.

An equally serious deficiency is the lack of real or simulated control groups to measure the impact of services. According to the law, clients chosen for reimbursed treatment should be those who are likely to leave benefit rolls with aid but not without it. Rehabilitation agencies seek trust-fund financing for those of their clients who are more likely to succeed. Persons under age 40 represented a seventh of disabled workers receiving insurance benefits in fiscal 1969. They were nearly a fifth of disabled worker beneficiaries rehabilitated without trust funds and nearly three-fourths of those rehabilitated with funds. A 1974 General Accounting Office study examined the cases of 350 persons who were rehabilitated and moved off social security disability rolls. In 51 percent of these cases, the individual had been scheduled for medical reexamination by the disability determination unit because of the possibility of recovery and regained earning capacity. Another 11 percent returned to work without receiving substantial rehabilitation agency services and should not have been counted. Using the methodology that yielded a 1.7:1 benefit/cost ratio for fiscal 1973, but excluding benefits from those not served or those possibly recovering on their own, the payoff would be reduced to 1.2:1.[14] If the subsequent national increase in recidivism rates had been factored into the calculations, the benefit/cost ratio would have been substantially less. And this still would not have accounted for creaming on the basis of education, previous earnings, age, and other variables related to success rates.

Lacking control groups, almost all vocational rehabilitation benefit/cost studies are seriously flawed. The studies have grown increasingly sophisticated in their efforts to get around this fundamental shortcoming, but they still overestimate the net impact of services. The return on the investment in the disabled may not be greater than that for helping other disadvantaged groups. This does not argue that vocational rehabilitation expenditures are unjustified. In a healthy economy the rate of return probably is substantial under the most conservative assumptions and using controls. But there is a great deal of uncertainty. If benefit/cost analysis is to be used to aid in policy decisions, then more realistic approaches are needed.

Client Priorities

The disabled range from functionally dependent quadraplegics to asthma sufferers. They include persons who have never worked, those with limited skills and education, others who are afflicted with transitional problems as they adjust to their disabilities, but some who are fully employed and drawing good salaries. In rationing scarce resources, a decision must be made whether to serve those with more serious physical and socioeconomic problems or to concentrate on those closer to the margin of successful employment. Different services are required or are feasible for different groups of clients. The chances of successful rehabilitation after such services vary.

Success Probabilities and Costs

The first step in setting priorities is to determine differential costs and success probabilities; this information is relatively straightforward. The next step, estimating and comparing the relative benefits and costs, is less clear-cut. The conclusions require guesses about what would have happened to different clients in the absence of services and how long their employment gains will last. If such determinations are difficult for programs as a whole, they are even more problematic for subgroups. The final step, assuming that relative benefits and costs are known, is to factor in value judgments. What priority should be given to efficiency considerations if they conflict with normative targets?

It is extremely difficult to analyze such questions. For instance, sheltered workshops concentrate on the most severely handicapped and the federal/state vocational rehabilitation program serves a mixed clientele, whereas veterans' programs serve a group that tends to have less severe problems. The institutional arrangements are completely different, the benefits and costs largely uncertain, and the normative issues conceptualized differently for each separate effort. Even within the federal/ state vocational rehabilitation program, comparisons are not easy.

Definition is a basic problem. To measure the relative effectiveness of services for the severely disabled, the selected group must be identified. The Rehabilitation Act of 1973 directed the Department of Health, Education and Welfare to develop a definition of the severely handicapped that would take into account the seriousness of mental or physical disabilities in terms of impairments to self-care, mobility, and self-direction as they affect employability and that would consider disabilities in terms of the requirements for multiple and extended rehabilitation services. The tentative definition concentrated on disabling conditions: it included persons with total blindness or blindness in one eye and a defect in the other, total deafness, loss of a limb because of orthopedic problems or amputation, psychosis, alcoholism, addiction, moderate or severe retardation, malignant neoplasms, diabetes, epilepsy, heart disease, and strokes. Those with lesser problems were excluded. In fiscal 1972, 31 percent of federal/state vocational rehabilitants were found to be within this definition of the severely handicapped.[15]

The chances of successful rehabilitation vary not only with disabling conditions but also with age, education, and other demographic factors. The rehabilitation rate among 35- to 44-year-old white males with nine to eleven years of education under the federal/state program in fiscal 1970 ranged from 66 percent for those with mental disabilities to 89 percent for those with genito-urinary difficulties. Among orthopedically handicapped males the success rates were—[16]

> Whites aged 35-44, 9-11 years of education—73 percent
> Nonwhites aged 35-44, 9-11 years of education—69 percent
> Whites under age 25, 9-11 years of education—80 percent
> Whites aged 35-44, 12 or more years of education—77 percent

The costs of services vary significantly among different client groups. In general, high costs are associated with the treatment of those with greater success probabilities.[17] Multiple regression analysis of 1970 national data revealed that, all else being equal, it cost $125 more to help 25- to 34-year-old rehabilitants than 45- to 54-year-olds, and $131 less for high school dropouts than for graduates. Successful rehabilitation of persons with orthopedic handicaps cost $374 more than that of the mentally retarded.[18]

Allocation of Scarce Resources

Because higher costs are sometimes incurred in treating those with greater success probabilities, benefit/cost ratios are not always correlated with rehabilitation rates. In fact, one major study comparing earnings gains and costs for different groups concluded that, if economic efficiency were to be taken as the criterion, it might be as desirable to focus on "the uneducated, the middle-aged, the severely disabled, the nonwhite, the unmarried and other low productivity groups as their more vocationally successful counterparts."[19] This study did not cross-classify education, age, race, and handicaps in any detail, and more technically sophisticated regression analyses produced opposite conclusions. One study using a number of variables and analyzing 1969 data for Florida concluded that it was less desirable on efficiency grounds to help older, unmarried, less educated, or severely disabled workers, although nonwhites apparently were a better investment than whites.[20] An even more detailed study using national fiscal 1970 data reached a similar judgment.[21] Another analysis, which compared all participants with the most severely handicapped as defined by the Department of Health, Education and Welfare on the basis of disabling conditions, found that—at a 7-percent discount rate—benefits were sixteen times costs for the program as a whole but only nine times for the severely handicapped.

The consensus reached by these benefit/cost regression analyses, however, does not prove that it is more cost-effective to serve the less disadvantaged. To begin with, the calculation of the marginal impact of a number of different variables on payoff rates is a useful exercise, but the approach more relevant to policymaking may be the simpler one of proceeding from cruder classifications. If most of the aged, for instance, have limited education and multiple impediments, the issue is whether on the average they will benefit from services, not whether age may have one effect and limited education another.

A more critical factor is that the assumptions used in estimating initial benefits and projecting them into the future are not neutral. Lower discount rates or more liberal assumptions about the continuance of gains will yield comparatively higher ratios for younger participants and for those experiencing a greater improvement at a higher cost. For instance, assuming a 3-percent annual increase in wages due to productivity gains and using a 4-percent discount rate, one study of 1970 national data found that the benefit/cost ratio (averaged for the different disabilities) for white males under age 25 with nine to eleven years of education was 30:1, compared with 10:1 for similar persons aged 55 and over. When a 2.5-percent productivity assumption and a 10-percent discount rate were used, the estimated ratios were 15:1 and 7:1 respectively. If attempts are made to simulate earnings changes based on the experience of other disabled workers of different ages, the relationships also change.

The average ratio for amputees, victims of neoplasm, and persons with blood and respiratory problems was double that for the mentally ill and retarded and persons with speech and hearing problems when gains were projected, assuming similar growth patterns for both groups, over time. When projections were based on the earnings of others with similar conditions, the ratios for the two groups were the same. The first set of assumptions suggested it would be much better to serve the first group, while the second set indicated that serving the mentally ill and retarded and victims of speech and hearing problems would be equally cost-effective.[22]

Without control groups or at least some refinement of benefit measurements and projection assumptions, benefit/cost analysis is of little help in determining the relative efficiency of serving different clienteles. Such analysis is a useful exercise: it illustrates that performance should not be judged by rehabilitation rates alone and that a stress on placement may not be functional; but it provides no clear answers. Even with refinements, serious limitations stemming from the basic uncertainties and complexities in rehabilitation persist. For instance, the criteria for disability insurance eligibility are relatively straightfoward and would seemingly identify persons with very limited potential. However, in 1976 the General Accounting Office, in a study that processed 221 sample claims in ten states, found that there was agreement among the states on acceptance, rejection or requests for additional documentation in only 23 percent of the cases. For instance, application denial rates ranged from 20 to 41 percent of the cases.[23]

Assessment of needs and potential is not an exact science, and attempts to dictate priorities by detailed national guidelines are bound to be frustrated by diverse local approaches. Yet, on the average, reduced or increased pressure on placement will influence behavior at the local level as will the provision or retrenchment of funds for services. The recent increases in the proportions of vocational rehabilitation clients found to be most severely handicapped may be in part a numbers game, but the make-up of client groups is changing and will continue to do so.

Whatever the cost-effectiveness of rehabilitating the more severely disabled, increased emphasis on serving them will mean that the average placement rate for the federal/state program as a whole will fall. Another result should be a reduced level of services per client. If, for instance, the feasible or standard mode of treating mental retardates costs half as much as treatment of the orthopedically handicapped, then the increased percentage of the former and falling percentage of the latter should result in a decline in average real costs per client. Yet, interestingly, service outlays rose over the last decade as the percentage of retardates grew while that of the orthopedically handicapped declined. Since services are valued at cost, it is difficult to assess the quantity or efficiency of delivery. But a rise in costs when a decline might have been predicted suggests the need for further investigation.

A falling rehabilitation rate is not an argument against serving the more severely disabled. Again, higher rehabilitation rates do not necessarily indicate higher benefit/cost payoffs. There is no rigorous basis for choosing between alternate clienteles. However, there are some reasonable grounds for questioning the current emphasis on the needs of the severely disabled.

First, structural and cyclical changes in the labor market have pushed the disabled further from the hiring door, so that the locus of most effective activity probably has to move forward along the labor queue. Second, the most severely disabled are most likely to have transfer income which alleviates need but complicates rehabilitation efforts. Third, a decline in the average future performance of vocational rehabilitation may adversely affect congressional support and lead to cutbacks or slower growth. Fourth, the acceptance of a more disadvantaged clientele will mean acquiescence to lower placement rates. The removal of the market test may have the adverse impact of disguising inefficiencies or increasing unnecessary services. For instance, the performance of the federal/state employment service deteriorated by most measures when it emphasized the hard-core unemployed in the 1960s. The vocational rehabilitation program apparently worked well in the last decade. But the economic recession compounded the difficulties of increasingly serving a clientele with more serious medical and economic problems. Unless the benefits are clear-cut, there are risks in tampering with an effective institution and trying to direct it to new goals.

The Service Mix

There are severe constraints on the overstated rhetoric of carte blanche treatment for the disabled under the federal/state vocational rehabilitation program. Resources are inadequate to provide everyone in need the services that would make them fully employable. Scarce resources must therefore be rationed among services, delivery institutions, and clients, with the aim of attaining the mix that will have the most favorable aggregate impact. Regrettably, little is known about the relative costs, impacts, and needs for different services.

Individual counselors make decisions based on their assessments of problems, knowledge of available resources, and some common-sense judgments about the effectiveness of different services, but they may have certain biases or respond sluggishly to changing conditions. They may also be maximizing performance within a framework that is ill designed for current needs and conditions. The available evidence raises some questions about the aggregate mix that results from counselors' separate decisions.

Content and Variability of Services

Counselors are central to the vocational rehabilitation process under both the veterans and federal/state programs, but little is known about their various functions. Studies of counselors' activities suggest that much time is spent in arranging services and processing paperwork rather than providing help and guidance. What the recipient regards as helpful frequently differs from what the vocational rehabilitation system considers most important. States vary markedly in their emphasis on counseling under the federal/state program. Maine, Massachusetts, Vermont, Arizona, Hawaii, and Oregon averaged fifteen rehabilitants for every counselor in fiscal 1975. In New Jersey, Kentucky, Mississippi, Tennessee, and South Carolina, the average caseload was sixty clients per counselor. The states with fewer clients per counselor achieved only 109 rehabilitations per 10,000 participants, compared with 273 in the states with less counseling input. In the states in which the caseloads were larger the rehabilitation rate per client served was 34 percent, versus 27 percent among the states with fewer clients per counselor. Whether the differences in performance are due to economies of scale or to other factors is uncertain; but if economies of scale are the answer, one would have expected that the rapid expansion of activity over the last decade could have been accomplished without a commensurate growth in the number of counselors. The number of cases served was two and one-half times higher in fiscal 1975 than in 1965, yet counseling man-years more than tripled, exclusive of the dramatic rise in counseling and evaluation work done in sheltered workshops. The number of rehabilitations per counselor man-year fell from forty-five in fiscal 1965 to forty-one in fiscal 1974 and to thirty-one in fiscal 1975, reflecting the sharply curtailed placement rate in 1975 and the rise from 8,387 to 9,963 man-years of counseling. Between 1967 and 1975 counseling and placement costs grew from 27 to 33 percent of total outlays.[24] Until it is proved that the services offered do make a difference, existing data raise serious doubts about the wisdom of expanded counseling and suggest that it may, in fact, be a candidate for retrenchment.

The emphasis on restoration services also varies markedly under the federal/state program. In ten states, less than a tenth of fiscal 1975 expenditures for individual services went for physical and mental restoration. In marked contrast, the proportion was over 40 percent in eight other states. Six states spent over 50 percent of restoration funds for surgery or treatment, but five others spent 25 percent or less. Connecticut, Utah, New Hampshire, and Kansas all used a seventh of individual service expenditures for restoration; in the first two states, more than six-tenths of it went for surgery and treatment, in the latter two, less than a third. Average costs also varied markedly.[25] Without medical expertise and some knowledge of the relationships between treatments and employability, it is difficult to say what is the ideal commitment.

"Training" covers a broad range of activities. College education is the primary emphasis of vocational rehabilitation for veterans. The constraints are the high cost of college, the amount of time involved, and its appropriateness for the most advantaged segment of the disabled population. But the benefits may be a permanent quantum leap in employability (although better documentation is needed before this judgment is accepted). Vocational training in technical schools or institutional skill centers can help the less educated. The problem is in bridging the gap between training and work. On-the-job training for the disabled has not been tried on any significant scale since the post-World War II period. The scattered recent evidence is mixed. Under the Job Opportunities in the Business Sector program, which subsidized employers to hire and train the disadvantaged, 4 percent of all participants in fiscal 1972 were handicapped. Their completion rate in that year was 46 percent, compared with 51 percent for the nonhandicapped. In the older on-the-job training effort under the Manpower Development and Training Act the disabled accounted for 11 percent of fiscal 1972 participants; they realized a completion rate of 60 percent, compared with 68 percent for the nonhandicapped. On-the-job training has the advantage of providing both "earning while learning" and a job at the end of training. The difficulties are in getting employers to participate and in ensuring that the persons hired are getting positions that otherwise would not be offered to them. Personal and vocational adjustment training accounted for 29 percent of training expenditures under the federal/state vocational rehabilitation program in fiscal 1975, but the content, much less the impact, remains unclear. Usually offered in sheltered workshops, training may merely prepare clients for their workshop assignments or may provide them benefits that are transferable into competitive employment. No one knows.

Once again, there is wide variance in the reliance on different modes of training. In six states, over half of the training funds under the federal/state program were devoted to college or university education. In contrast, over half the funds in four other states were spent on personal and vocational adjustment. Less than 4 percent of funds nationwide went for on-the-job training, but three states spent proportionately four times as much. [26]

Strategies for creating jobs range from sheltered workshops to public employment. Workshops provide opportunities for those who have limited options. If the aim is work experience that will lead to competitive employment, then it is being achieved for only a small minority of participants. If the aim is to supplement income and provide constructive activity at less cost than income transfers and recreation programs, then workshops are generally succeeding. The handicapped were also hired under the Emergency Employment Act of 1971 and subsequent job-creation programs. These were supposed to be transitional jobs, usually at entry-level government salaries. No evidence is available on how well the handicapped did relative to the nonhandicapped.

The Proper Recipe

The federal/state vocational rehabilitation program demonstrates that many roads lead to Rome. The fifty states offer as many different models of possible service levels and mixes. There is no way to know which is most appropriate for each situation or what the implications are for the optimum overall service mix.

About the only thing that can be done is to try to pin down the relationships between certain approaches and changing background factors. Job creation makes sense in a slack labor market. To the extent the more severely handicapped are served, the need increases for sheltered workshop opportunities. If the needs of a more select clientele are emphasized, transitional jobs in the public sector would be desirable.

Flexible supported-work programs, now being tested for such disabled groups as addicts and alcoholics, are another possibility. In a tight labor market, on-the-job training might receive greater play, perhaps in the form of a special national subsidy program for employers hiring the handicapped. This would be most effective if combined with affirmative antidiscrimination efforts. To the extent that the creation of jobs lessens the need for counseling and restoration, such services can be targeted for those who cannot perform in available slots.

These observations stop far short of identifying an ideal service mix. In the absence of hard evidence, judgments must be based on "gut feelings" about the nature of the problems and the promise of different approaches. Since the employment perspective begins by concentrating on labor markets and the vocational dimensions of rehabilitation, it is perhaps not surprising that this perspective would end up favoring greater emphasis on job creation and development. There is evidence, however, that the majority of potential clients support this priority. Among those disabled or previously disabled in 1972 who had received services from any source, 71 percent reported receiving physical therapy or special devices, but only 28 percent received what they considered vocational services. Yet when all the disabled and previously disabled (including previous recipients of aid) were asked what services they currently wanted, 67 percent of those with needs wanted vocational assistance, and only 20 percent requested physical therapy or special devices. Among the recovered still desiring services, less than a tenth needed restoration, but four-fifths wanted vocational assistance.

The message is not simply that restoration is being over-emphasized or that the socioeconomic handicaps of the disabled should receive more attention. Rather, it is that current restoration and manpower efforts for the disabled will have a greater impact if more attention is paid to the jobs that may eventually be secured. This means more than merely gearing up manpower services for the disabled. A central criticism of manpower programs in the late 1960s and early 1970s was that they reflected excessive optimism in the potential of human resource development. Critics, focusing on the labor market impediments faced by the disadvantaged, raised doubts about whether the programs were generally able to lift participants into better paying career opportunities. The prescription was job creation plus antidiscrimination and other institutional changes. These policy recommendations apply equally well to vocational rehabilitation programs. The disabled, who are at the end of the labor queue, need special assistance in overcoming institutional barriers and reestablishing or establishing lasting job connections. Training and other services must be linked with jobs. Subsidies and job-creation programs can be used as mechanisms to change institutions. Greater focus is needed on placing the disabled in better jobs in which they can sustain their independence without falling back on relief. There must be a renewed commitment to the primary goal of vocational rehabilitation, which is self-supporting employment.

Macroeconomic Considerations

The health of the economy affects everyone, but the impacts are greatest for the groups in the labor force that are least prepared for or capable of work and least desired by employers. This includes the disabled. From 1963 to 1969 employment grew a vigorous 15 percent, and the number of unemployed fell by 30 percent. In the subsequent six years the growth in employment declined to 9 percent, and unemployment rose by 177 percent. Jobs were not available for many skilled and educated workers, but they were even scarcer for the more disadvantaged—the aged, the deficiently educated, and minorities. The employment rate of civilian 45- to 64-year-old males declined overall from 88.3 percent in 1969 to 81.3 percent in 1975 while falling only slightly for younger males. The labor force participation rate fell 1.5 percentage points for white males but 5.4 percentage points for nonwhites. The rate for college-educated males aged 35 to 44 rose slightly between March 1968 and March 1974 but declined for those with less than a high school education.

Even in the 1960s, however, the favorable effects of tight labor markets did not outweigh the combined impacts of higher minimum wages, technological change, and increased credentials requirements, which made the unskilled and inexperienced workers expendable. Despite the increased availability of jobs, the difference in employment rates between male 35- to 44-year-old college graduates and those with nine to eleven years of schooling widened from 1.1 to 2.2 percentage points between 1962 and 1969. The gaps widened similarly between the rates for white and nonwhite males, and for older and prime-age workers. The lean years of the 1970s merely accelerated these trends, or at least eliminated the compensatory increase in jobs.

These economic and labor force developments are best explained by the labor queue theory. Workers can be ranked according to their employability, which is a combination of their productive capabilities—as manifested in previous job experience, training in job skills, and formal education—and their attractiveness to employers, whether based on objective standards or on biases. Those at the end of the line are much more likely to be jobless, much more likely to drop out of the labor force, and much less likely to find well-paying jobs. Some persons with limited education and experience or with undesirable characteristics, such as a criminal record, may achieve great success, and a college diploma or previously steady work is no guarantee against failure. But success probabilities are determined largely by demographic and work experience characteristics.

The level of aggregate demand determines how far back down the labor queue employers will reach to fill their needs. In a tight labor market the more skilled and desirable workers are not available, and employers have to be less selective. Those at the end benefit disproportionately in good times, since they are the source of labor that must be tapped for expansion. When aggregate demand declines, however, the last hired become the first fired, losing out in the competition with more attractive workers.

Human resource investment programs aim to increase the productivity of those at the end of the line, thereby raising their success probabilities. Antidiscrimination efforts, job restructuring, and other measures try to alter employers' standards and practices that are unrelated to productivity. Employment programs seek to create jobs that may not be warranted on the basis of productivity alone but can be justified by the benefits to the individual and to society in reduced transfers combined with productive output.

At the End of the Queue

The labor queue notion is a fruitful approach to understanding the problems of the disabled, who are more likely than the nondisabled to be older, black, and with limited education—characteristics that are obstacles to employment even without physical or mental impairments. Moreover, in each age, sex, race, and educational attainment cohort, disabled workers have lower earnings and lower labor force participation rates. Employers prefer nondisabled workers, even if disadvantaged, to the disabled. There is also a queuing within the universe of the disabled. The chances of being severely disabled are related to the types of disabling conditions; mental illness and retardation clearly have the most negative consequences.

The substantial annual inflow and outflow from the disabled universe is also explained by the labor queue notion. The chances of becoming disabled are highest and exit probabilities lowest for those with unsteady work experience, limited education, greater age, and more severe handicaps. The key to continued labor force participation is the ability to remain in the same job after the onset of the disabling condition, and this is quite clearly affected by whether the employer is hiring or laying off workers and whether the disabled employee is considered valuable to the firm.

The impacts of labor market changes are evidenced by the sharp increase between 1966 and 1972 in the proportion of disabled persons unable to work regularly or at all regardless of the severity of functional limitation. The decline in work was greatest for those with the most serious physical and mental problems. The older cohorts and persons with limited education were hardest hit. As economic conditions deteriorated in the

97

mid-1970s, the employment status of the disabled unquestion-ably suffered even more. Between 1971 and the third quarter of 1975, the number of persons aged 16 to 59 outside the labor force because of illness or disability rose from 2.4 million to 2.9 million, while the number among those claiming to want a job rose from 425,000 to 537,000.

Implications of Slack Labor Markets

The continuing high unemployment in the mid-1970s has important implications for vocational rehabilitation efforts. First, the composition of the universe of need has changed. Added to those with obvious work impediments are many disabled who have less severe handicaps, who would be able to find jobs and work productively in normal times. For these, medical treatments will be less critical, since it is labor market changes that have pushed them out of the work force.

Second, deteriorating economic conditions reduce the absolute and relative success probabilities of the disabled, dispropor-tionately affecting the most severely handicapped and disad-vantaged. The employer who is willing to hire the disabled consequently has a greater selection and will undoubtedly choose those with less limiting handicaps. For example, the mentally retarded, who have a slim chance of finding work in the best of times, will be competing with the orthopedically handicapped, who under normal conditions would be employed and are generally preferred by employers.

Third, the relative effectiveness of various service strategies is affected by labor market changes. In a booming economy on-the-job training, job development, antidiscrimination action, and direct placement can be used to gain access to jobs for the disabled. These approaches will obviously have a reduced payoff when unemployment rises; when there are not enough jobs, work experience and public employment programs make more sense. By the same token medical treatment, which may be adequate to lift many above the employability threshold in a tight labor market, may not be enough to ensure success when this threshold rises in a recession. The notion that almost anyone can be made employable by intensive services must be reexamined when the competition for jobs becomes stiff and millions of nondisadvantaged workers are idle.

Fourth, hard times will force many who would otherwise be employed onto disability and relief rolls. Once the attachment to the labor force is broken and a person gets into the welfare system, complications arise in getting him or her back into the job market. A worker who earns a livelihood may disdain dependency, may view welfare as a complex, forbidding system, and may not realize the full extent of benefits. But once a person is forced to depend on transfers, values may change, and work may be the alternative that is viewed with apprehension, given the probability of losing welfare benefits. The serious recession in the mid-1970s and the concomitant growth of transfer caseloads probably moved a significant portion of the disabled out of the work force permanently.

Fifth, a slack labor market probably reduces the benefit/cost ratio of rehabilitation services while altering the relative payoff in serving different clienteles. The average disabled client has a slim chance of employment without services, and a slack labor market can reduce these success probabilities very little. But the success rate after services, which is normally high, can fall precipitously as placement becomes more difficult. The net payoff therefore declines.

These are probable, not proven, impacts of the 1970s economic slump. Data on the disabled and on vocational rehabilitation programs are too limited, and their interpretation is too uncertain, to prove anything. For instance, past studies comparing the fifty states have not documented any significant relationship between vocational rehabilitation placement rates and unemployment. In fact, a few found that performance indicators rose rather than fell when unemployment increased, apparently as better qualified persons were screened into the program.[27] The problem with such cross-sectional studies is that there is so much variance in the incidence and nature of disability, in the characteristics of the labor market, and in rehabilitation institutions that it is difficult to sort out the effects of unemployment. Further, the cross-sectional variation is small compared with recent cyclical changes. The fact that individual states can adjust to different conditions over the long run does not mean that a rise in unemployment nationwide does not have an effect. It clearly does. The ratio of successful to unsuccessful closures under the federal/state program declined from 3.40:1 for 1964 through 1968 to 3.07:1 during the subsequent four years.[28] It then dropped precipitously to 2.75:1 in 1974 and 2.28:1 in 1975. But these figures tell only part of the story. The performance of vocational rehabilitation depends also on the duration of benefits. The ballooning recidivism rate of rehabilitants previously terminated from disability insurance rolls demonstrates a dramatic decline in job retention, which probably affects all previous rehabilitants.

Given this evidence supporting the theoretical probability that the disabled are seriously affected by labor market changes, policy adaptations would seem to be appropriate. Employment and training programs for the disadvantaged offer examples of possible changes. Public employment and work-support efforts were expanded in response to the growing job deficit in the 1970s. In 1975 these efforts cost $3 billion, amounting to a fivefold increase since 1971. Meanwhile, outlays for training and placement declined (after adjusting for cost-of-living changes). Job creation increased from one-fifth of manpower outlays in fiscal 1971 to almost one-half in fiscal 1975 as total outlays doubled. There was also a noticeable shift to a less disadvantaged and better educated clientele.

In contrast, vocational rehabilitation policies were slow to adjust to changing conditions. While the recession probably doubled the number of nonworking disabled persons between the late 1960s and the mid-1970s, federal/state vocational rehabilitation expenditures rose by less than two-fifths between 1971 and 1975. There was no major shift from training or medical services to public employment. The number of clients in certified sheltered workshops rose by 50,000 in the early 1970s, but expansion stopped in the face of the severe recession at mid-decade. Moreover, this growth was largely financed under the guise of reimbursing evaluation and training in workshops, rather than as a straightforward funding of sheltered work.

If macroeconomic developments have had the postulated effects on the disabled, then vocational rehabilitation policies should be brought more in line with general manpower policies. This would include a deemphasis of service strategies designed to increase employability, an emphasis on job creation and work experience efforts, and a higher priority on the less severely rather than on the more severely disabled. Although it is to be hoped that unemployment will decline in the late 1970s, it is doubtful that those at the end of the labor queue will ever again be as well off as in the 1960s. Every recession in the past has had a permanent effect on structural problems, and the subsequent recoveries have failed to restore the most severely disadvantaged to their old status. Different priorities and policy responses may therefore be needed over the long run. There are no easy answers and no certainties, but economic conditions must be given much greater consideration in the formulation of vocational rehabilitation policies.

Workfare and Welfare

Social insurance and welfare benefits are a major source of support for those with curtailed earnings. In 1971 half of all disabled households received public support (table 14). Social security aided nearly a fourth; one in seven received welfare benefits, one in ten veterans' compensation. Social insurance benefits averaged $2,100 annually per recipient unit, public assistance $1,500. Together they accounted for an eighth of the aggregate income of households with a disabled adult and for almost a fourth of those with a severely disabled adult. Since household survey data tend to undercount transfer payments substantially and since the dollar totals do not include in-kind aid, such as subsidized medical care and housing, food stamps, social services, and other assistance, the importance of government assistance is even greater.

Growth of Income Support

Income support programs have been growing rapidly, and the disabled have become more and more dependent on such

Table 14. Transfer Income of Disabled and Nondisabled Households, 1971

Source of income	Percentage receiving			Mean income from source for recipients			Percentage of total income		
	Disabled	Severely disabled	Non-disabled	Disabled	Severely disabled	Non-disabled	Disabled	Severely disabled	Non-disabled
All transfers	47.6	63.2	18.9	$2,076	$2,256	$1,446	12.3	22.9	2.3
Social Insurance and service-based	38.6	49.7	17.1	1,997	2,248	1,417	9.6	18.0	2.0
Social security	23.0	36.0	4.9	1,712	1,711	1,814	4.9	9.9	0.7
Railroad disability	0.6	1.0	0.1	2,167	2,171	2,690	0.2	0.3	–
Veterans' compensation	10.3	12.4	4.8	1,385	1,630	1,114	1.8	3.3	0.4
Workers' compensation	3.3	3.6	1.5	1,410	1,750	504	0.6	1.0	0.1
Government employee benefits	3.8	5.4	1.3	3,291	3,240	3,130	1.6	2.8	0.3
State temporary disability	0.7	0.4	0.3	607	1,132	608	0.1	0.1	–
Unemployment compensation	5.0	3.4	6.1	879	1,065	750	0.5	0.6	0.4
Public Assistance	14.1	20.8	2.3	1,544	1,474	1,339	2.7	4.9	0.3
Aid to the blind and aid to the permanently and totally disabled	5.6	9.5	0.2	1,270	1,209	1,161	0.9	1.8	–
AFDC	5.3	6.8	1.6	2,041	1,895	1,499	1.3	2.1	0.2
Other	4.0	5.9	0.6	988	1,078	734	0.5	1.0	–

SOURCE: Social Security Administration, U.S. Department of Health, Education and Welfare, 1972 survey of the disabled, unpublished tabulations.

programs. In 1965, 47 percent of household units with a severely or occupationally disabled adult member reported receiving transfers. (Those with secondary work limitations are excluded, since their number changed significantly between 1966 and 1972 and their problems are less serious.) By 1971 the proportion aided rose to 55 percent. The numbers are not strictly comparable because households with two disabled persons (which are therefore most likely to rely on public welfare) were counted once in 1966 and twice in 1972; still there was a substantial increase. A better indication is provided by transfer program data. The number of reported recipients of disability insurance benefits and of public assistance for the blind and totally disabled increased by two-thirds between 1966 and 1972, while expenditures more than tripled. In the next three years the combined caseload rose by another two-fifths, or by a greater absolute number than between 1966 and 1972 (table 15).

Table 15. Public Assistance for Disabled Persons, Fiscal 1966, 1972, and 1975

| | Source of assistance | | | |
	Total	Aid to the blind	Aid to the permanently and totally disabled	Disability Insurance
Number (thousands)				
1966	2,642	84	588	1,970
1972	4,398	80	1,068	3,250
1975	6,234	74	1,860	4,300
Expenditures (millions)				
1966	$ 2,129	$ 85	$ 487	$1,557
1972	7,251	1,005	1,393	4,853
1975	11,645	1,284	3,158	7,203

SOURCE: *Social Security Bulletin,* September 1976, tables M-22 through M-32.

The disability insurance total includes dependent family members. But the number of disabled workers alone rose from 1.1 million in December 1966 to 1.8 million in December 1972 and to 2.5 million three years later. If the number of severely and occupationally disabled remained roughly constant between 1972 and 1975, as it did during the previous six years, this would mean that the percentage receiving benefits more than doubled. The growth rate of disability insurance is also accelerating, with 600,000 acceptances in 1966, 1.0 million in 1972, and 1.3 million in 1975.

Several factors contributed to this rapid growth. Legislative changes opened the doors to new claimants. Under the disability insurance program, the definition of disability was changed in 1965 to include all incapacities expected to last a year or longer, whereas the previous definition had been restricted to those of "long-continued and indefinite duration." In that year and in 1967, restrictions were eased for the younger blind, widows, and recipients of workers' compensation benefits. In 1972 the waiting period was reduced from six to five months. The black lung program was initiated in 1969 and significantly liberalized in 1972; by the end of 1975 it was providing benefits to nearly 500,000 ex-miners at a total cost of almost $900 million annually. In 1974 Aid to the Blind, Aid to the Totally and Permanently Disabled, and Old Age Assistance were replaced by the Supplemental Security Income (SSI) program, which introduced federal definitions of disability and, by footing more of the bill, encouraged states to expand benefits.

Another likely growth factor was the "greening" of the welfare and social insurance system, partly the result of court decisions and partly the result of changing attitudes in the welfare establishment. A major 1960 court decision held that disability determination under disability insurance required consideration not only of what the individual could do but also of available employment opportunities. Decisions had previously been made on the basis of medical analysis of functional capabilities, but the court held that the theoretical ability to engage in substantial gainful activity was not enough if no reasonable employment opportunities were available. To re-establish the priority of medical factors in disability determination Congress changed the law in 1967, defining substantial gainful work to include any job existing in the national economy, whether or not job vacancies were available locally. Yet the door could not be closed.

In 1967, 70 percent of the 466,000 cases requiring determination of disability were allowed. When the number of determinations rose to 852,000 by 1973, including more marginal cases, the preliminary approval rate fell to 63 percent, but court decisions and a greater number of reversals held the final acceptance ratio nearly stable. Furthermore, roughly 75 percent of determinations in 1975 were made on the basis of age, education, and work experience, compared with only 10 percent in 1963. Medical factors are considered necessary, but the other conditions have become increasingly important over time. [29]

The improvement in benefits undoubtedly was a major cause of growth. Between 1966 and 1975 the average monthly benefit for the disabled worker more than doubled from $98 to $216, exceeding the rise in prices by one-third and the increase in real hourly earnings by one-fourth. In 1966 Medicaid and Medicare were just getting started. Food stamps were limited to a few pilot projects, and there were few units of subsidized housing. By 1975 food stamp use was widespread, and disability recipients were eligible for Medicaid on the basis of low income and for Medicare after two years on the rolls. Subsidized housing doubled. The total benefit package available to transfer dependents, in short, improved dramatically.

Economic developments also were of great importance. Disability insurance is directed to those who cannot achieve substantial gainful employment, whereas public assistance is distributed on the basis of need and rather strict proof of physical limitations. When disabled persons were forced out of work by rising unemployment, they qualified for aid and in many cases had no other recourse.

Transfers as Work Disincentives

Yet the expansion of income support might also be the cause rather than the effect of reduced employment if the disabled reacted to more attractive benefits or expanded eligibility by shunning work. To the extent this is the case, the changing

105

employment patterns might reflect a pull rather than a push out of the labor market and therefore might not be indicative of reduced employment opportunities for those willing and able to work.

There is a substantial difference between the work propensities of income transfer recipients and nonrecipients. A third of severely disabled males without disability insurance benefits were working in 1972, four times the percentage among beneficiaries; 11 percent of unaided females with severe handicaps had jobs, compared with 4 percent of recipients. The question however, is whether disability insurance merely aided those who were unable to work, or whether it encouraged marginal workers to leave the labor market.

Regression analysis of 1966 data suggested that, all else being equal, those with transfers worked less. Each $100 increase in annual transfers reduced the labor force participation rate by an estimated 0.6 percent for prime-age white males and by 1.1 percent for white males aged 55 to 64. For blacks the percentages were higher. An increase in real benefits of 33 percent, say from $1,500 to $2,000 (roughly comparable to that occurring between 1966 and 1975) would reduce the labor force participation rate by 3.0 percent for disabled prime-age white males and by 5.5 percent for prime-age blacks. As noted previously, the labor force participation rate for severely and occupationally disabled males potentially qualifying for disability insurance declined by a sixth between 1966 and 1972 alone, so that benefit level changes accounted for only a minority of the drop in participation.

Other calculations using 1966 data found that, for each increase of 10 percent in the ratio of benefits to average monthly wage in the last job, the chances of application rose 2.4 percent.[30] If this were the case, the 25-percent increase in benefits relative to wages between 1966 and 1975 would have increased the likelihood of application by 6 percent; in fact, the increase in the incidence of application has far exceeded this amount.

Such calculations are inconclusive, since cross-sectional relationships do not necessarily apply over time and since there have been changes in the disability transfer system as well as in the extent of in-kind aid. Yet the data seem to support the common-sense judgment that the rise in disability rolls was not just the result of improved benefits and increased dependency propensities, but also the result of declining job opportunities.

Rehabilitation Instead of Relief

If employment opportunities were readily available for those receiving government transfers, it might be possible to help recipients prepare for jobs and to get them back to work. This has not proved easy, however.

Reimbursements for rehabilitation services from the disability insurance trust fund have been authorized since 1965 to get recipients back to work and off assistance. Up to 1 percent of disability payments could be used for this purpose initially, 1.5 percent a decade later. Through fiscal 1974, $218 million was spent on reimbursements; $83 million was available in fiscal 1975. An estimated 300,000 beneficiaries received reimbursed services through fiscal 1974, and 75,000 in fiscal 1975. Reimbursements are also authorized from general revenues for rehabilitation services to SSI recipients, although only 3,600 were served in fiscal 1975. Under workers' compensation, rehabilitation may also be financed by private insurance or provided by referral to the public programs. According to scattered evidence, probably less than 5 percent of clients receive vocational rehabilitation.[31]

Are rehabilitation services a way to slow the growth of transfer program caseloads? The disability insurance experience raises doubts. Reimbursed services are reserved for beneficiaries who could be expected to return to competitive employment long enough so that savings from benefits will exceed rehabilitation costs. Earnings of $200 monthly are prima facie evidence of the ability to carry on substantial gainful employment, and those who reach this level of earnings face a possible cutoff of benefits. To mitigate the work disincentives, there is a year-long trial work period before termination, and terminees who lose their jobs are automatically eligible for benefits again. Yet persons with earnings potential of only $2,400 annually and

107

about the same level of benefits are not likely candidates for services. The system apparently favored the less disadvantaged as candidates for rehabilitation services.

Even among these selected clients, the success rates have been modest. Among the 52,000 trust-fund-financed cases served in fiscal 1973, 12,000 were closed, two-fifths of these unsuccessfully; only 2,600 reimbursed rehabilitants were terminated from the rolls. Performance had deteriorated markedly as a larger proportion of recipients were drawn into rehabilitation efforts and as unemployment rose in the early 1970s. The cost per rehabilitant rose from $2,200 in fiscal 1969 to $3,400 in fiscal 1973, while the cost per terminee increased from $6,300 to $15,300. There was also substantial substitution of disability insurance reimbursements for regular vocational rehabilitation expenditures. Total terminees declined as a proportion of disability beneficiaries from 2.3 percent in fiscal 1970 to 1.6 percent in fiscal 1973, while the number of service-reimbursed recoverees fell from 0.17 to 0.11 percent. As noted previously, the minor reductions in the welfare rolls achieved through fiscal 1973 were reversed during the next two years as many were forced back into dependency. This is not encouraging. There is little evidence that vocational rehabilitation can play a major role in countering the growth of disability insurance rolls.

The interrelation of workfare and welfare for the disabled is not unique. In many ways, the 1970s explosion in disability benefits mirrored the earlier experience with welfare. In the late 1960s, AFDC caseloads rose at an accelerated rate as a result of legislative changes, court decisions, liberalization of the welfare establishment and, most important, the improvements in welfare benefits relative to real wages. Welfare was blamed for causing family breakups and for encouraging marginal workers to leave the labor force. Public support fell as costs increased, and the so-called welfare mess was perceived as a major domestic crisis. Early efforts to halt growth through absolute ceilings, work incentives, and training services had little effect. Eventually the hard line was taken—tracking down absent fathers, policing more carefully against abuse, making mandatory referrals to jobs and, most important, holding the line on benefits.

Disability programs have been cushioned by the public's greater acceptance of aid for those with obvious mental or physical handicaps, but recent caseload increments have probably included persons with less serious problems who do not evoke as much sympathy. Exposure of such disability "cheaters" may undermine the credibility of the system. Work incentives are already an issue under disability insurance and workers' compensation, and there is likely to be some experimentation with other benefit formulas. Training has been expanded in hopes of stemming caseload growth, and public disappointment is likely if this does not occur. If costs continue to rise, policymakers might well adopt a "get tough" stance.

The Lessons

Are there any lessons that can be learned from the past to avoid further mistakes and disappointments? Experience suggests that, among those at the end of the labor queue who are affected by declining job opportunities and attracted by the higher benefit floor, employment is not a realizable objective for more than a small minority. No doubt some of the welfare mothers who could have found work preferred public assistance; but for most, jobs were not available or work was not a feasible option. It proved difficult to sort out who should be served and who were the loafers. Most of all, however, it proved difficult to find jobs even after training. Public employment was not the answer because the public sector was just as leery of aid recipients as the private sector. The recession further reduced the chances of employment. The Work Incentive Program (WIN), which provided training and other services, may have been a worthwhile investment, but it hardly made a dent in welfare rolls and was tarnished because of this failure. In brief, the employment problems of those who turn to income support tend to be very severe and very difficult to treat.

A second lesson is that tinkering with the benefit system is not likely to increase employment greatly. The substantial gainful-employment cutoff of $200 monthly earnings under disability insurance allows a recipient to keep everything up to this amount and still get a disability insurance check but cuts off benefits if earnings rise a dollar more (although this rarely occurs in practice). The answer would seem to be to introduce incentives as under WIN, in which the recipient retains the first $30 of monthly earnings plus one-third of the remainder and the amount of all work-related expenses without offset. Yet after WIN became effective in the late 1960s, work rates among welfare mothers did not increase noticeably. The only effects were to improve the status of recipients already working, and to open the doors to others whose earnings had previously made them ineligible. To change the disability definition by allowing substantially higher earnings, or to permit recipients to keep a portion of their earnings, would break down the notion of disability and would expand eligibility to the less seriously handicapped.

A third lesson is that growth will not necessarily continue exponentially. In the 1960s welfare levels were raised, and substantial in-kind benefits were added, improving the welfare package to the poverty level. Combined with liberalizations in eligibility standards, the effect was to make welfare a reasonable option for large numbers of female-headed families; within a few years most got on the welfare rolls. But the near-saturation of the eligible population and the stabilization of real benefits halted growth even in the face of a major recession. The boost in disability benefits under the Supplemental Security Income program likewise resulted in a spurt of recipients. As the recession levels off, as the universe of need is saturated, and as real benefits are raised less rapidly, the increase in disability beneficiaries is likely to slow down. Patience and compassion may be better policy than an aggressive effort to reform the disability system, to expand rehabilitation efforts, or to "get tough" with applicants.

4

Diagnosis and Prescriptions

Based on evidence of severe needs among those with mental and physical handicaps, bolstered by public compassion, and supported by claims of significant effectiveness, vocational rehabilitation has expanded rapidly. This expansion, without the benefit of critical assessment, has been essentially independent of other human resource development efforts. The problems of the disabled have been viewed as unique, demanding special and separate treatments.

Causes and Cures

Without challenging the notion that there are differences between the disabled and other disadvantaged groups in the labor force or the idea that specialization in the delivery of services is worthwhile, it appears that the problems of disability and the prospects of vocational rehabilitation programs would benefit from an assessment based on a broad perspective.

The Employment Perspective

Socioeconomic and physical handicaps tend to overlap. The disadvantaged and disabled share problems of limited education and job skills, as well as discrimination. Those at the end of the labor queue are affected disproportionately by structural and cyclical changes in the labor market. Having low income, they are strongly affected by income support policies.

Inasmuch as both groups compete for limited resources and scarce job opportunities, the problems of the disabled must be considered in conjunction with those of the disadvantaged, and the effectiveness of vocational rehabilitation and general manpower programs should be judged by comparable standards. Such policy issues as the scale or mix of services, the clientele, and the overlap with income support should be resolved consistently, with recognition of commonalities as well as differences.

The population whose labor market activities are impaired by physical and mental impediments is, on the average, older, more frequently nonwhite, less educated, and less skilled and has less work experience than the nondisabled population. The compounding of physical or mental and socioeconomic handicaps leaves the disabled at the very end of the labor queue. Yet there is a minority among the disabled at any given time who have higher employment potential. The inflows and outflows from the disabled universe are substantial, and exit probabilities are greatest for the least disadvantaged.

Assuming a relative constancy in the prevalence of physical or mental conditions, changes over time in the employment status of the disabled are determined largely by the availability of jobs and by changes in income support policies. The disabled at the end of the labor queue have been deeply affected in the 1970s by structural shifts in the economy and by high unemployment. Large numbers have left the labor force altogether, and income support programs have expanded to take care of them.

Rehabilitation Efforts

Public vocational rehabilitation efforts have been growing rapidly. Annual combined caseloads tripled between 1965 and 1975, and real expenditures nearly quadrupled to $1.7 billion.

During this decade the separate programs reported serving a combined total of over 5 million clients. The disabled, when surveyed, report much lower participation totals. The disparity is partly due to double-counting, but many clients no doubt received only minimal services. Even if the totals are inflated, however, it is clear that vocational rehabilitation is a major commitment that affects a significant segment of the disabled.

The traditional federal/state vocational rehabilitation program is the cornerstone of the system. It provides or purchases a wide range of services based on rehabilitation plans developed for each client. The service mix has remained relatively constant, with expenditures about equally split between counseling and placement, physical restoration or training, and other services, plus administration. In 1975 outlays amounted to $800 per service recipient, $2,800 per rehabilitant. Three of four participants were successfully rehabilitated, substantially improving earnings and employment from entry to exit, although there are questions in some cases about the extent to which the services contributed to improved employability and about the duration of benefits. The program functions as a screening mechanism, selecting the potentially most employable from the eligible groups. In the last decade, however, there has been an increased emphasis on the more severely disabled, and the trend was accelerated by 1973 legislation that sanctioned this priority. It is uncertain whether the program can continue to expand and to emphasize the more severely disabled in a slack labor market. Performance, as measured by competitive placement rates and costs per placement, will in all likelihood deteriorate.

Rehabilitation services for veterans are offered as compensation and do not have to be justified by the criterion of public benefits exceeding public costs. Almost all the clients are disabled males in their prime working years. In contrast to the federal/state vocational rehabilitation program, priorities were altered in 1974 to aid more veterans with minor physical or mental limitations. The emphasis is on college education, but the disabled are offered extensive individual services, financial support, training, and job development assistance; the estimated annual cost per individual served is at least six times that of the federal/state vocational rehabilitation program. Although follow-up data are meager, it appears that disabled Vietnam-era veterans who availed themselves of vocational training benefits had lower unemployment and dropout rates than those not trained. There is also evidence that a college education can offset some of the effects of disability; the value of the sheepskin was unequivocally demonstrated for World War II disabled veterans, although the payoff of a college degree may not be as great for today's veterans.

Sheltered workshops are a vital component of the vocational rehabilitation system, providing work experience and, in many cases, long-term employment (albeit at subminimum wages) for the most seriously handicapped. Although workshops have proliferated since the early 1960s, growth has recently leveled off as a result of several factors. As the productivity of clients fell further and further behind competitive norms, workshop viability was maintained by cutting relative wages and increasing outside subsidies. But rates of pay can hardly be lowered further and still justify workshops as employment mechanisms, nor are expanded subsidies for evaluation and training justified by the placement record of workshops. They have increasingly become service institutions that deliver medical, counseling, and vocational assistance. Staff salaries, in fact, dwarf the earnings of clients. Yet the effectiveness of workshops in improving well-being or vocational potential, except for the fact that they do provide sheltered work, remains unproven. It might be better to subsidize wages instead of services, although improved cost accounting and performance measures are needed before accepting such a conclusion.

Critical Issues

One of the critical issues underlying these diverse rehabilitation efforts is estimation of the universe of need. The adequacy of resources must be measured against some standard, and the larger the deficit between services and needs the greater the justification for expansion. Usually generated by vocational rehabilitation advocates, needs estimates have been inflated by the inclusion of many who cannot feasibly be served, who are not interested in services, or who do not need them because they already have adequate employment or good chances of improvement. Some analysts have documented service deficits by confusing the total stock of disabled with the annual increment in need. Under conservative definitions it can be demonstrated that the capacity of vocational rehabilitation programs exceeds the annual incremental needs. This is not a criticism, however: additional facilities may help reduce the stock of the disabled or might offset the effects of worsening economic conditions that may increase the need. More liberal and readily available aid or changes in priority to serve either the most severely or the marginally disabled would, of course, expand the universe, since there will always be takers for free services. Nevertheless, the nation apparently is much closer than many believe to doing what is currently mandated in a comprehensive fashion.

Human resource development programs, including vocational rehabilitation, are based on the notion that the efforts will improve employability and result in long-run benefits to society and the individual. One way to assess effectiveness is to compare the potential value of these benefits with the service costs to determine whether the investment has a positive rate of return. Benefit/cost analysis has played a significant role in judging absolute and relative performance. Most studies have found benefits far exceeding costs for vocational rehabilitation; ratios have been substantially above those for general manpower programs. Favorable findings have generated momentum for the expansion of vocational rehabilitation even while manpower programs were being retrenched and reformed. Yet these analyses are suspect. They have relied on comparisons of earnings immediately before and after rehabilitation, rather than comparing participants with matched samples of disabled nonparticipants over an extended period. Since many of the disabled recover or improve their employment status without services and since those who are more likely to improve are selected for the program, before-and-after comparisons exaggerate the impact of rehabilitation efforts. Calculations with and without control groups have demonstrated that the differing methods used in assessing vocational rehabilitation and manpower programs were responsible for the differing performance assessments. It is uncertain whether vocational rehabilitation pays off either absolutely or relatively as a human capital investment; chances are that it does both, but success is not as clear-cut as most existing studies would suggest.

Macroeconomic developments are having a major impact on the disabled. There has been a precipitous decline in the number and proportion who are employed; many who would normally work despite their physical or mental handicaps cannot find jobs. This increases the overlap between disability and welfare. A slack labor market undermines antidiscrimination, job development, placement, and on-the-job training efforts. It increases the need for public employment or sheltered work. The relative payoffs in serving different clienteles probably are also altered. As the severely handicapped are moved further and further from the hiring door, the chances of eventual competitive placement are reduced, so that a less seriously disabled clientele will need to be served. The vocational rehabilitation system was slow to adjust to the changing economic scenario in the 1970s.

The disabled are a diverse group, ranging widely in severity of physical and economic conditions. Given scarce resources, a fundamental question is who among the possible claimants is to be served. There has been no consistent overall policy. In sheltered workshops and the federal/state vocational rehabilitation program the long-run trend has been to aid the more severely handicapped; the veterans' program, in contrast, was opened to the less disabled by 1974 changes in the law. Benefit/cost estimates for different groups have suggested that the payoff is higher for the less severely disabled, but the methodologies bias the comparisons in unknown directions. One thing is certain, however: if those with less vocational potential are served, rehabilitation and placement rates will eventually fall, which would have ramifications on the entire rehabilitation system.

The optimal service mix remains an uncertainty. The marginal impact of particular treatments on different clients is unknown.

Only a few general observations and a cataloging of questions are possible. Intake and assessment methods are more art than science, and they vary from counselor to counselor. The use of weighted formulas to influence client selection promises to complicate the situation. Counseling is a major part of all programs, but much of what goes by this name may be paperwork and administration rather than the provision of services to the disabled clients. Training for the disabled ranges from work experience to subsidized college education. Sheltered work fits in with public preferences, but it has yet to be proved that a job at subminimum wages is particularly therapeutic or rehabilitative. Institutional training of the disabled has uncertain results, and on-the-job training has been used only sparingly. The returns to higher education for the disabled probably are significant but are not well documented. Placement and job development have received very little emphasis in the federal/state vocational rehabilitation program or in sheltered workshops, and antidiscrimination efforts have not been pushed.

The increased incidence of income transfers raises other issues. Disability insurance, the black lung program, workers' compensation, and Supplemental Security Income have been expanding dramatically, suggesting the possibility that the disabled are being pulled rather than pushed from the work force. There have been some efforts to counter rising caseloads with rehabilitation services. These seemed to be effective at first but, as the economy slumped and the scale of activity rose, performance fell off precipitously. Experience with the rising AFDC rolls in the late 1960s and early 1970s suggests that neither training nor work incentives are likely to make much difference, and that expansion will level off once benefits stabilize at an acceptable real level and the eligible universe becomes saturated.

Policy Considerations

These issues, programs, and problems are very complex, defying simplification into a straightforward agenda of policy prescriptions. Yet the preceding analysis does suggest some policy considerations.

117

First, rapid growth in any institution involves expanded frills and unnecessary overhead, and there is reason to believe that vocational rehabilitation efforts have not escaped such developments. A rigorous assessment of rehabilitation institutions to ensure that waste is eliminated and that clients are served efficiently is overdue.

Second, nonvocational assistance—such as counseling, evaluation, homemaker training, and varied social services—could probably be trimmed without affecting chances for gainful employment. This is most clearly the case in sheltered workshops. Nonvocational services may be justified and indeed necessary on their own grounds, but the impacts must be more clearly documented, especially since the persons prescribing the needs are those delivering the services.

Third, jobs might be given greater emphasis. If the severely disabled are to be served, sheltered workshop opportunities can be expanded by subsidizing employment and wages directly. Supported work and public employment programs could help the better qualified among the handicapped. Subsidized on-the-job training in the public sector might be tried if the labor market tightens and if antidiscrimination efforts are mounted. Under all programs, employer outreach efforts are needed, and placement services might be strengthened.

Fourth, the emphasis on the more severely disabled should be reexamined. This is a complex issue that involves many value judgments. There are millions of persons with serious disabilities and severe needs who can benefit from help. In the face of the limited employment potential of the most severely handicapped and the considerable resource investment needed to prepare them for gainful employment, consideration might be given to whether they might be better served with income support, so that scarce rehabilitation resources can be focused on others who might be helped more in the labor market.

Fifth, vocational rehabilitation should not be relied upon as the major strategy to counter rising welfare and disability insurance caseloads. It may function well at the margin, but its potential is limited for those with handicaps so severe that they can qualify for transfer aid.

The purpose of this analysis is not to redirect policy, but to suggest different perspectives for decisionmakers. Labor market conditions must be a primary consideration in assessing efforts on behalf of the disabled. There must be a greater understanding of the overlap between disability and other obstacles that prevent workers from functioning effectively in the work force. The role of vocational rehabilitation in the galaxy of human resource development efforts must be recognized, policies coordinated, and experience cross-fertilized. There is no doubt about the importance of vocational rehabilitation in combating the consequences of disability, but there is room for improvement—and it will best be realized by taking a new look at old problems.

Notes

Chapter 1

1   Urban Institute, *Report of the Comprehensive Service Needs Study* (Washington: Urban Institute, 1975), pp. 311–318.

2   James A. Colbert, Richard A. Kalish, and Potter Chang, "Two Psychological Portals of Entry for Disadvantaged Groups," *Rehabilitative Literature*, July 1973.

3   Urban Institute, *op. cit.*, pp. 321–325.

4   Lawrence D. Haber, "Disabling Effects of Chronic Disease and Impairment—II, Functional Capacity Limitations," *Journal of Chronic Disability*, 1973, p. 129.

5   *Ibid.*, pp. 127–151.

6   *Ibid.*, pp. 139–140.

7   Monroe Berkowitz, *et al.*, *Measuring the Effects of Disability on Work and Transfer Payments* (New Brunswick: Rutgers University Press, 1972), pp. 171–194.

8   Saad Z. Nagi, *An Epidemiology of Disability Among Adults in the United States* (Columbus: Mershon Center, Ohio State University, 1975), pp. 12–15.

9   Ralph Treitel, "Onset of Disability," *Social Security Survey of the Disabled, 1966*, Report No. 18 (Washington: U.S. Department of Health, Education and Welfare, Social Security Administration, June 1972).

10   *Ibid.*, p. 17.

11   Edward Steinberg, "Work Adjustment of the Recently Disabled," *Disability Survey 71, Recently Disabled Adults*, Report No. 3 (Washington: U.S. Department of Health, Education and Welfare, Social Security Administration, January 1976), pp. 19–22.

12   *Ibid.*, p. 35.

13   Pearl S. German and Joseph W. Collins, "Disability and Work Adjustment," *Social Security Survey of the Disabled, 1966*, Report No. 24 (Washington: U.S. Department of Health, Education and Welfare, Social Security Administration, July 1974), pp. 1–33.

14   Social Security Administration, U.S. Department of Health, Education and Welfare, "Disability Survey 1969, Follow-up of Disabled Adults," unpublished tabulations.

15 Mathematica Policy Research, *A Longitudinal Study of Unemployment Insurance Exhaustees* (Princeton: Mathematica, Inc., 1976), p. 30.

Chapter 2

1 Rehabilitation Services Administration, U.S. Department of Health, Education and Welfare, "Statistical Notes No. 6: Length of Time Spent in Referral and Applicant Statuses by Selected Groups of Clients Whose Cases Were Closed During Fiscal 1967" (mimeo.), December 1967.

2 Rehabilitation Services Administration, U.S. Department of Health, Education and Welfare, "Statistical Notes No. 30: Major Disabling Conditions of Clients of State Vocational Rehabilitation Agencies Whose Cases Where Closed During Fiscal Year 1970" (mimeo.), June 1972.

3 Rehabilitation Services Administration, U.S. Department of Health, Education and Welfare, "Information Memorandum RSA-IM-75-28" (mimeo.), November 1975.

4 Abt Associates, *The Program Services and Support System of the Rehabilitation Services Administration* (Cambridge, Mass.: Abt Associates, Inc., 1974), pp. 213–215.

5 Cited in Abt Associates, *op. cit.*, p. 83.

6 *Ibid.*, pp. 213-215.

7 U.S. General Accounting Office, *Effectiveness of Vocational Rehabilitation in Helping the Handicapped* (Washington: U.S. Government Printing Office, 1973), p. 26.

8 Abt Associates, *op. cit.*, p. 236.

9 *Ibid.*, p. 219.

10 Rehabilitation Services Administration, U.S. Department of Health, Education and Welfare, "Information Memorandum RSA-IM-74-26" (mimeo.), November 1974.

11 Rehabilitation Services Administration, U.S. Department of Health, Education and Welfare, *State Vocational Rehabilitation Agency Program Data*, Fiscal 1968, 1971, and 1975 (Washington, 1969, 1972, and 1976).

12 Rehabilitation Services Administration, U.S. Department of Health, Education and Welfare, *Characteristics of Clients Rehabilitated in Fiscal Years 1968–1974* (Washington, 1974); and "Information Memorandum RSA-IM-75-28," (mimeo.), November 1975.

13 Rehabilitation Services Administration, U.S. Department of Health, Education and Welfare, "Information Memorandum RSA-IM-75-22" (mimeo.), August 1975.

14 Rehabilitation Services Administration, U.S. Department of Health, Education and Welfare, "Information Memorandum RSA-IM-76-63," March 1976.

15 Rehabilitation Services Administration, U.S. Department of Health, Education and Welfare, "Information Memorandum RSA-IM-75-28," November 1975.

16 Abt Associates, *op. cit.*, p. 181.

17 Joseph Greenblum, "Evaluating Vocational Rehabilitation Programs for the Disabled: National Long-Term Follow-Up Study," *Social Security Bulletin*, October 1975, p. 10.

18 Frederick C. Collignon and Richard Dodson, *Benefit-Cost Analysis of Vocational Rehabilitation Services Provided to Individuals Most Severely Handicapped* (Berkeley: Berkeley Planning Associates, 1975), p. 14.

19 Abt Associates, *op. cit.*, pp. 196–201.

20 Cited in Abt Associates, *op. cit.*, pp. 167, 249.

21 U.S. General Accounting Office, *op. cit.*, p. 30.

22 Abt Associates, *op. cit.*, pp. 233–234.

23 Sar A. Levitan and Karen Cleary, *Old Wars Remain Unfinished* (Baltimore: Johns Hopkins University Press, 1973), pp. 30–45, 146–154.

24 Administration of Veterans Affairs, *Annual Report 1974* (Washington: U.S. Government Printing Office, 1975), p. 188.

25 Thurlow R. Wilson, John A. Richards, and Deborah H. Berein, *Disabled Veterans of the Vietnam Era: Employment Problems and Programs* (Alexandria, Va.: Human Resources Research Organization, 1974), tables IV-14 and IV-15.

26 U.S. Veterans Administration, unpublished tabulations from survey of disabled Vietnam-era veterans by Wilson, Richards and Berein.

27 *Ibid.*

28 Wilson, Richards, and Berein, *op. cit.*, p. 93.

29 Thrainn Eggertsson, *Economic Aspects of Higher Education Taken Under the World War II GI Bill of Rights* (Columbus: Ohio State University, 1972), tables 17 and 20.

30 Wilson, Richards, and Berein, *op. cit.*, pp. 107–176.

31 Greenleigh Associates, *The Role of Sheltered Workshops in the Rehabilitation of the Severely Handicapped* (New York: Greenleigh Associates, 1976), vol. II, p. 26.

32 *Ibid.*, vol. III, pp. 38–79.

33 William H. Button, ed., *Rehabilitation, Sheltered Workshops, and the Disadvantaged* (Binghamton, N.Y.: Vail-Ballou Press, 1970), pp. 22–27.

34 Greenleigh Associates, *op. cit.*, vol. III, p. 145.

35 Employment Standards Administration, U.S. Department of Labor, 1972, unpublished tabulations.

36 Greenleigh Associates, *op. cit.*, vol. II, pp. 145–146.

37 *Ibid.*, pp. 123, 143, 151.

38 *Ibid.*, pp. 77–101.

39 Urban Institute, *Report of the Comprehensive Service Needs Study* (Washington: Urban Institute, 1975), pp. 529–533.

40 Greenleigh Associates, *op. cit.*, vol. II, p. 185.

41 Button, *op. cit.*, pp. 3–79, and Greenleigh Associates, *op. cit.*, vol. II.

Chapter 3

1 These studies are summarized and standardized in Monroe Berkowitz, *An Evaluation of the Structure and Functions of Disability Programs* (New Brunswick: Rutgers University Press, 1975), pp. 188–196.

2 U.S. General Accounting Office, *Effectiveness of Vocational Rehabilitation in Helping the Handicapped* (Washington: U.S. Government Printing Office, 1973).

3 Edward Steinberg, "Work Adjustment of the Recently Disabled," *Disability Survey 71, Recently Disabled Adults*, Report No. 3 (Washington: U.S.

Department of Health Education and Welfare, Social Security Administration, January 1976), tables 1–5.

4   Joe Nay, John Scanlon, and Joseph S. Wholey, *Benefits and Costs of Manpower Training Programs: A Synthesis of Previous Studies with Reservations and Recommendations* (Washington: Urban Institute, 1971), p. 11.

5   These studies are carefully analyzed in Larry L. Kisner, "A Review of Benefit/Cost Analysis in Vocational Rehabilitation," *Supplemental Studies for the National Commission on State Workmen's Compensation Laws* (Washington: U.S. Government Printing Office, 1973), vol. II, pp. 383–396.

6   Monroe Berkowitz, *et al., Measuring the Effects of Disability on Work and Transfer Payments* (New Brunswick: Rutgers University Press, 1972), pp. 188–196.

7   Frederick C. Collignon and Richard Dodson, *Benefit-Cost Analysis of Vocational Rehabilitation Services Provided to Individuals Most Severely Handicapped* (Berkeley: Berkeley Planning Associates, 1975).

8   Abt Associates, *The Program Services and Support System of the Rehabilitation Services Administration* (Cambridge, Mass.: Abt Associates, Inc., 1974), p. 260.

9   David J. Farber, "Changes in the Duration of Post Training Period in Relative Earnings Credits of Trainees," U.S. Department of Labor, Employment and Training Administration, August 1971 (unpublished).

10   Joseph Greenblum, "Evaluating Vocational Rehabilitation Programs for the Disabled: National Long-Term Follow-Up Study," *Social Security Bulletin*, October 1975, p. 10.

11   Committee on Ways and Means, U.S. House of Representatives, *Committee Staff Report on the Disability Insurance Program* (Washington: U.S. Government Printing Office, 1974), pp. 303–304.

12   *Ibid.*

13   *Ibid.*

14   U.S. General Accounting Office, *Improvements Needed in Efforts to Rehabilitate Social Security Disability Insurance Beneficiaries* (Washington: U.S. Government Printing Office, 1975).

15   Collignon and Dodson, *op. cit.*, pp. 18–19.

16   Berkowitz, *op. cit.*, pp. 321–325.

17   Donald M. Bellante, "Multivariate Analysis of a Vocational Rehabilitation Program," *Journal of Human Resources*, Spring 1972, p. 230.

18   Berkowitz, *op. cit.*, pp. 328–339.

19   Ronald Conley, "A Benefit/Cost Analysis of the Vocational Rehabilitation Program," *Journal of Human Resources*, Spring 1966, pp. 226–252.

20   Bellante, *op. cit.*, pp. 236–240.

21   Berkowitz, *op. cit.*, p. 342.

22   *Ibid.*, pp. 350–352 and 368–370.

23   Subcommittee on Social Security, Committee on Ways and Means, U.S. House of Representatives, statement by Gregory J. Ahart, February 1976.

24   Rehabilitation Services Administration, U.S. Department of Health, Education and Welfare, *State Vocational Rehabilitation Agency Program Data, Fiscal Year 1975* (Washington, 1976), pp. 2–30.

25   *Ibid.*

26   *Ibid.*

27   Abt Associates, *op. cit.*, p. 81.

28 Rehabilitation Services Administration, U.S. Department of Health, Education and Welfare, *Caseload Statistics, State Vocational Rehabilitation Agencies, 1973*, p. 11.

29 U.S. General Accounting Office, *Improvements Needed;* and Committee on Ways and Means, *Report on Disability Insurance Programs*, pp. 275–315.

30 Monroe Berkowitz, William G. Johnson, and Edward H. Murphy, *Policy and the Determinants of Disability* (Princeton: Rutgers University Press, 1975), table I-IV and p. 229.

31 National Commission on State Workmen's Compensation, *Compendium on Workmen's Compensation* (Washington: U.S. Government Printing Office, 1973), p. 162.

Index

Activity limitations, 14–15

Age: of disabled veterans, 54; of disabled workers, xi, 7; and physical handicaps, 7, 11, 18; of rehabilitants, 42; and work disability, 7, 11, 18, 81, 105

Aid to Families with Dependent Children (AFDC), growth of, xi

Aid to the Blind (AB), 27; to blind veterans, 51; public grants for, 63; workshops for, 60–62. *See also* Supplemental Security Income program (SSI)

Aid to the Totally and Permanently Disabled (APTD). *See* Supplemental Security Income program (SSI)

Benefit/cost ratios, 76–84, 86–90; in analyzing performance, 115; decline of savings to expenditures in, 83; and discount rates, 77, 87; of enrollees under Manpower Development and Training Act (MDTA), 78–81; methodology for, 78–81; regression analyses of, 87; and use of control groups, 84, 88

Control groups: and benefit/cost ratios, 84, 88; in manpower programs, 78–81, 83; need for, 47–48, 116; structure of, 76; use of, 76, 78–79

Counseling, x, 33, 90–91; and administration of services, 90; costs of, 40; of disabled veterans, 50; and performance of rehabilitants, 91; for rehabilitation, 35, 37–38, 91; in sheltered workshops, 91

Counselors: activities of, 38, 91; clients per counselor, 91; number of, 91; and rehabilitations, 91; and the system, 90

"Creaming": definition of, xi–xii; standards for, 36

Delivery of services, 30–40; costs of, 40, 47, 76, 82; deficits in, 73–75; effectiveness of, 85–86, 89, 94, 98; extent of, 35, 75; primary responsibility for, 31–35, 73; types of, 37, 73

Disability. *See* Work disability

Disability insurance: attitudes toward, 109; earnings under, 109, 115; eligibility for, 88, 104–7, 110;

125

Library of Congress Cataloging in Publication Data

Levitan, Sar A.
    Jobs for the disabled.

    (Policy studies in employment and welfare; no. 28)
    Includes bibliographical references and index.
    1.   Handicapped—Employment—United States.   2.   Voca-
tional rehabilitation—United States.   I.   Taggart,
Robert, 1945-   joint author.   II.   Title.
HD7256.U5L48   331.5'9'0973   76–49910
ISBN 0–8018–1925–3
ISBN 0–8018–1926–1 pbk.

DATE DUE

DEC 2 2 1997					

DEMCO, INC. 38-